HOTSPOTS
JAMAIC

GW00374871

Written and updated by Polly Rodger Brown
Original photography by Mark Bassett

Published by Thomas Cook Publishing
A division of Thomas Cook Tour Operations Limited
Company Registration no. 3772199 England
The Thomas Cook Business Park, Unit 9, Coningsby Road
Peterborough PE3 8SB, United Kingdom
email: books@thomascook.com, Tel: + 44 (0) 1733 416477
www.thomascookpublishing.com

Produced by Cambridge Publishing Management Limited
Burr Elm Court, Main Street, Caldecote CB23 7NU

ISBN: 978-1-84848-180-0

First edition © 2007 Thomas Cook Publishing
This second edition © 2009
Text © Thomas Cook Publishing
Maps © Thomas Cook Publishing/PCGraphics (UK) Limited

Series Editor: Adam Royal
Production/DTP: Steven Collins

Printed and bound in Spain by GraphyCems

Cover photography © Alamy/Richard Broadwell

CONTENTS

WHAT'S IN YOUR GUIDEBOOK?

Independent authors Impartial up-to-date information from our travel experts who meticulously source local knowledge.

Experience Thomas Cook's 165 years in the travel industry and guidebook publishing enriches every word with expertise you can trust.

Travel know-how Thomas Cook has thousands of staff working around the globe, all living and breathing travel.

Editors Travel-publishing professionals, pulling everything together to craft a perfect blend of words, pictures, maps and design.

You, the traveller We deliver a practical, no-nonsense approach to information, geared to how you really use it.

● *Total tranquillity in Ocho Rios*

INTRODUCTION
Getting to know Jamaica

Jamaica

Caribbean Sea

Ann's
y

Ocho
Rios

Port Maria

A3

Annotto Bay

Highgate

A1

C

instead

A4

John Crow & Blue
Mtns National Park

Port Antonio

R Grande

Blue Lagoon

A3

Hope Botanical
Gardens

Blue Mtns
Blue Mt Peak
▲
2256

John Crow Mtns

Spanish
Town

KINGSTON

A2

Fort
Clarence

A4

Old
Harbour

Port
Royal

Norman Manley
International

Yallahs

Morant
Bay

*Folly
Bay*

N

Getting to know Jamaica

Jamaica is the third-largest island in the Caribbean, with a land mass of 11,424 sq km (4,411 sq miles). Its closest neighbours are the larger islands of Cuba and Hispaniola. Jamaica is 234 km (145 miles) in length from west to east, while the distance from north to south at the island's widest point is 80 km (51 miles).

There are three distinct landscapes in Jamaica. The first is the Blue Mountain range, above Kingston in eastern Jamaica, whose highest peak reaches 2,256 m (7,402 ft). Apart from the mountains, the most

● *The beautiful setting of Port Antonio*

dramatic scenery in Jamaica is Cockpit Country, a remote area of the northwest where eroded limestone (karst) has created a series of sinkholes, caves and caverns. The coast is a series of picturesque beaches and coves that are most developed on the island's north coast and remain largely unspoilt in Portland, Jamaica's eastern region.

Jamaica is semi-tropical, with a year-round average temperature of 27°C (80°F). May to October is the rainy season when it's slightly hotter and very humid. Hurricanes are most likely in October, and several have devastated the island, most recently Hurricane Dean in 2007.

Life is hard for most Jamaicans, with very low weekly wages (on average 7,000 Jamaican dollars, or J$, equivalent to £60 or US$88) and a high cost of living. Many people work in large, all-inclusive hotels where hours are very long and wages minimal. The growing number of these hotels, largely owned by foreigners, has meant that many local tourist businesses struggle to survive. Nevertheless, Jamaicans, who are always well turned out, are known for their laughter, good spirits and warmth.

It was in 1494 that Christopher Columbus arrived in Jamaica, known as 'xaymaca' (land of wood and water) by the Taino Indians who inhabited it; they were rapidly wiped out by the harsh treatment and European diseases of their Spanish colonisers. In 1655 the English captured the island from the Spanish, covering it in lucrative sugar plantations and importing West African slaves to work on them. Jamaica became independent from Britain on 6 August 1962, though it remains part of the Commonwealth. After a period of political turmoil in the 1970s, the country now has a stable democracy and a Labour prime minister, Bruce Golding.

The long-standing popularity of cricket in Jamaica has been surpassed in recent years by football. The national team, known as the Reggae Boyz, has a large and noisy following.

Christianity is very important to Jamaicans, and churches are packed on Sundays. Jamaica also has its own religion, the Rastafari movement, whose dreadlocked members aim to live close to nature, usually avoid meat and believe that smoking ganja (marijuana) is sacred.

THE BEST OF JAMAICA

Jamaica, with its high mountains, lush tropical vegetation, myriad winding rivers and white-sand beaches, is one of the most dramatically beautiful islands in the Caribbean. For those looking for a break from sun, sea and sand, there is a wide variety of natural beauty spots to visit inland as well as a rich cultural life, mostly based around sport, music and religion.

TOP 10 ATTRACTIONS

- **Climbing waterfalls** Where waterfalls meander over layers of rock, climb upriver for an exhilarating experience (see page 105).

- **The Marley legend** Indulge in Marley-mania at the Reggae Xplosion Museum in Ocho Rios (see page 25) or the Bob Marley Museum in Kingston (see page 40).

- **Watching the sun set in Negril** The western tip of Jamaica is the best spot to watch the sun slide into the sea in a blaze of pinks, oranges and reds (see page 56).

- **Hiking in the Blue Mountains** The tranquil paths and tracks that wind through the coffee farms and pine groves of the mountains are well known to the locals – take a guide with you (see page 75).

- **Rafting down the Rio Grande** Reclining on a flower-decked bamboo raft while being punted along a wide, calm river is the most peaceful day out imaginable (see page 105).

- **The luminous lagoon** On clear moonlit nights the algae in this small lagoon near Falmouth are lit up like fireflies and swimmers leave long luminous trails in the water (see page 66).

- **Cranbrook Flower Forest** A lovingly tended garden near Ocho Rios on the north coast is filled with orchids, lilies and other exotic blooms (see page 69).

- **Port Royal** Once the haunt of pirates, Port Royal is an atmospheric town with a ruined fort and excellent fish restaurants (see page 79).

- **Crocodile safari** The large crocodiles along the Black River are known by name to the boatmen who take tourists on nature tours (see page 47).

- **Appleton's Rum Factory** Find out how Jamaica's favourite drink is made and sample the best of it afterwards (see page 87).

◗ *Soak up the sounds on this music-loving island*

SYMBOLS KEY

The following symbols are used throughout this book:

ⓐ address **ⓣ** telephone **ⓕ** fax **ⓦ** website address
ⓛ opening times **ⓝ** public transport connections **ⓘ** important

---

The following symbols are used on the maps:

𝒊	information office	**○**	city
✉	post office	**○**	large town
▣	shopping	**○**	small town
✈	airport	**▨**	POI (point of interest)
✚	hospital	**—**	main road
♟	police station		minor road
†	church	**- -**	national park
❶	numbers denote featured cafés, restaurants & evening venues		

RESTAURANT RATINGS

The following symbols after the name of each restaurant listed in this guide indicate the price of a typical three-course meal without drinks for one person. Remember that lunch or a set menu will often be cheaper.

£	under J$1,200
££	J$1,200–J$2,400
£££	over J$2,400

▶ *A palm-shaded massage hut in Bloody Bay*

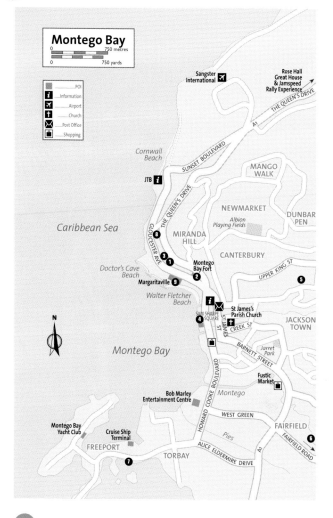

Montego Bay

Jamaica's second city, Montego Bay was aptly named 'El Golfo de Buen Tiempo' – the Gulf of Good Weather – by Christopher Columbus when he sailed into its calm turquoise waters in 1494. Established during the 1940s and 1950s as a place to restore health and vitality, Mo'Bay (as it's known to the locals) is a busy tourist resort with a wide range of accommodation and a rapidly growing international airport that brings people directly to the 'island in the sun' from the US, Canada and Europe. Set around a gently curved stretch of famously fine white sand and clear sea and backed by green hills, the city is divided into two distinctive parts.

The 'Hip Strip', Gloucester Avenue, is an easily negotiated 2.4-km (1½-mile) thoroughfare that runs between the city centre and the airport and is fronted by Montego Bay's two loveliest beaches and several large, all-inclusive resorts. Here, within walking distance, are most tourist facilities – hotels, bars, restaurants, souvenir shops and taxi ranks – and visitors need never leave the area. It takes them just a few minutes to get from their hotel rooms to the sea and to a host of places where they can have a great meal or a cool drink: the small distances between everything on Gloucester Avenue are a big attraction for holidaymakers. Tourist police parade the Strip regularly to keep hustlers at bay.

The bustling downtown area of Montego Bay has a lot of fascinating history. Its centre is Sam Sharpe Square, named after a Baptist minister who led a slave rebellion in 1831 and was hanged as a punishment. His statue depicts a fiery preacher, Bible in hand, and is situated here in memoriam. In one corner of the square is The Cage, built in 1806 as a jail for runaway slaves and drunken sailors. Nearby is St James's Parish Church, built in the late 18th century, which has some marble statuary and fine stained-glass windows. Tourists who venture downtown should be careful to hold onto their belongings – petty theft is not unknown.

In the hills overlooking Montego Bay, many wealthy Jamaicans have built large villas. A string of luxury, all-inclusive hotels line the island's north coast for around 10km (6 miles) east of the city. There are a number of Great Houses (the grand mansions of sugar plantation owners) to visit and several excellent golf courses.

BEACHES

Doctor's Cave Beach

It was the gently curving stretch of fine white sand and clear aquamarine sea of Doctor's Cave Beach that first brought tourists in sizeable numbers to Montego Bay. In the early 20th century, a British physician claimed that taking the waters here, a beach supposedly fed by a natural spring, cured all manner of ailments. People flocked from abroad to try it for themselves.

These days Doctor's Cave is a private club with a small entrance fee and all amenities – changing rooms, showers, beach umbrellas, deckchairs and lilos (to rent at an additional cost) and various watersports activities. There are several restaurants and bars that serve cold drinks, lunchtime snacks and full meals. The most popular of these is The Groovy Grouper Beach Bar & Grill.

ⓐ Gloucester Ave, opposite the Gloucestershire Hotel ⓣ 952 2566
ⓦ www.doctorscavebathingclub.com ⓛ 09.00–17.00 daily
ⓘ Admission charge

Walter Fletcher Beach (Aquasol Theme Park)

Walter Fletcher Beach is another attractive spot, again with fine white sand and clear water. It has a livelier atmosphere than Doctor's Cave, with longer opening hours. It appeals more to families, children and young people, and sports fans. It has a wide range of activities – go-karting, tennis, sea trampolines and watersports – as well as satellite

JTB (JAMAICA TOURIST BOARD)

ⓐ Cornwall Beach ⓣ 952 4425 ⓦ www.visitjamaica.com
ⓛ 08.30–16.00 Mon–Fri, 09.00–13.00 Sat, closed Sun

◆ *Take a glass-bottomed boat from Walter Fletcher Beach*

television tuned invariably to sporting events or MTV, chairs and umbrellas to rent and lockers for valuables. The Voyage Sports Bar & Grill serves up hot dogs, burgers and Jamaican favourites such as jerk chicken and patties. At weekends and on holidays there are often music events – live bands and DJs – on the beach.

ⓐ South end of Gloucester Ave, close to downtown ❶ 979 9447/940 1344 ⓦ www.aquasoljamaica.com ⓛ 09.00–19.00 Mon–Fri, 09.00–22.00 Sat & Sun ❶ Admission charge

THINGS TO SEE & DO

Jamspeed Rally Experience

Keen car fans now have an opportunity to test their skills on the island's best dirt circuit. Souped-up rally cars – Peugeots, Mitsubishis and Subarus – race around at high speed, for up to three hours, dust flying and brakes screeching. Nervous drivers can participate in the Co-Drivers Experience when professionals do all the hard work and the thrill belongs to everyone.

ⓐ Spot Valley Entertainment Complex, Rose Hall ❶ 953 0744 ❶ Advance reservations necessary

Margaritaville

Ask tourists who've been to Mo'Bay what they enjoyed most and they'll probably say Margaritaville. Not just a waterfront bar and restaurant, Margaritaville Montego Bay was the first in a highly successful chain of venues island-wide. At Margaritaville you can soak up the sun on its rooftop deck or enjoy the outdoor whirlpool. You can jump onto the water-slide and, after several twists and turns, shoot out into the sea below where there are water trampolines. You can pick from dozens of different cocktails and be entertained by the all-singing, all-dancing bar staff. There's American-style food – burgers, tortilla wraps, fried chicken, key lime pie – as well as top sports action on satellite television, plus a gift shop. Themed party nights – toga, karaoke, beach wear – keep the action going until the small hours, even though the doors open just after breakfast. It's all very cheesy but great fun.

ⓐ Gloucester Ave ⓣ 952 4777 ⓦ www.margaritavillecaribbean.com
ⓛ 10.30–03.00 daily

Rose Hall Great House

Rose Hall sits above the North Coast Highway, a gleaming white mansion in expansive grounds. It was built in the 1770s, when the sugar industry was at its height in Jamaica, by plantation owner John Palmer, but the house was abandoned in the 19th century and left to go to rack and ruin. The house was bought in the 1960s, and its present American owner has spent a lot of money bringing it back to its original state. The walls of the house are lined in silk fabric (a faithful replica of an original design made for Marie Antoinette) and its rooms are filled with substantial pieces of antique furniture made by renowned craftsmen Sheraton, Chippendale and Hepplewhite.

◔ Rose Hall Great House

Rose Hall, though impressive in its own right, is best known for the legend of Annie Palmer, one-time mistress of the Great House, who is said to stalk its marble halls even now. The story goes that she murdered three husbands, took a multitude of slave lovers and was found strangled in her bed. There is little evidence to substantiate all the rumours, but Jamaicans love the myth and ghost hunting goes on occasionally at the house.

ⓐ Rose Hall, North Coast Highway ❶ 953 2323 Ⓦ www.imexpages.com/rosehall ❸ 09.00–18.00 daily ❶ Admission charge

Water fun

A handful of catamarans ply the coast of Montego Bay every morning and at sunset on popular 'booze cruises' where the rum punch flows, the reggae is cranked up to top volume and the boat handlers try to persuade tourists to dance their socks off. Most boats leave from Pier One on downtown's seafront highway, Howard Cooke Boulevard or Doctor's Cave Beach.

There are two local and reliable charter companies, **Dreamer Catamaran Cruises** (❶ 979 0102 Ⓦ www.dreamercatamarans.com) and **Jamaica Watersports** (❶ 281 3229 Ⓦ www.jamaicawatersports.com).

TAKING A BREAK

Cafés & restaurants

Jamaica Bobsled Café £ ❶ Excellent hearty pizzas, sandwiches and cocktails in a cheerful centrally located café. ⓐ 69 Gloucester Ave ❶ 940 7009 ❸ 11.00–02.00 daily

Pork Pit £ ❷ Long-standing jerk place with a choice of excellent spiced meat and fish, served up fast-food style. ⓐ 27 Gloucester Ave ❶ 952 1046 ❸ 11.00–23.00 daily

Calypso Gelato ££ ❸ Delicious ice cream in a multitude of flavours. Cakes also. ⓐ 75 Gloucester Ave ❶ 979 5172 ❸ 10.00–19.00 daily

Pier One ££ ❹ Surf 'n' turf-style eatery with fabulous setting on the waterfront. Children's menu, sandwiches, wraps and burgers for lighter lunches. ⓐ Howard Cooke Blvd ❶ 952 2452 ❷ 10.00–23.00 daily

AFTER DARK

Richmond Hill ££ ❺ Great spot for a sunset drink – the views are stupendous and the hotel terrace is very elegant. ⓐ Richmond Hill, Union St ❶ 952 3859 ❷ 11.30–14.30 & 17.30–21.00 daily

Day-O Plantation £££ ❻ Special romantic atmosphere with poolside dining and sophisticated international menu. ⓐ Fairfield ❶ 952 1825 ❷ 18.00–24.00 daily

Houseboat Grill £££ ❼ Unique setting on moored houseboat with classy international cuisine and happy-hour cocktails. Booking essential. ⓐ Southern Cross Blvd, Montego Freeport ❶ 979 8845 ❷ 18.00–22.00 daily

Nightlife
Coral Cliff ££ ❽ Mo'Bay's slot-machine kingdom also has live bands, karaoke nights, cabaret and several places to eat and drink. ⓐ 165 Gloucester Ave ❶ 952 4130 ❻ www.coralcliffjamaica.com ❷ 24 hours daily

Margaritaville ££ ❾ The main event in Mo'Bay, Margaritaville (see page 18) is its most popular tourist attraction. ⓐ Gloucester Ave ❶ 952 4777 ❻ www.margaritavillecaribbean.com ❷ 10.30–03.00 daily

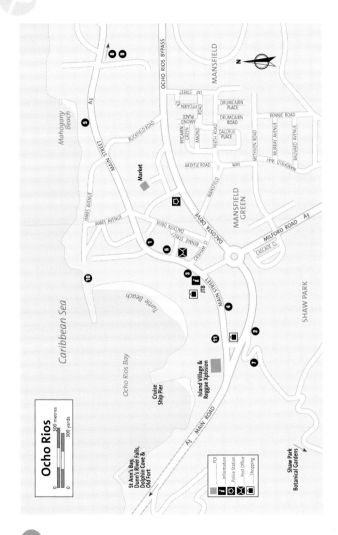

Ocho Rios

Ocho Rios

Ocho Rios (known locally as 'Ochi') was once a sleepy fishing village so named on account of its plethora of waterfalls (the name derives from the Spanish '*chorreros*', meaning 'gushing waters'). The Spanish used the area as a stronghold to fight the English and there are several historic sites commemorating the battles that marked their last stands.

In the 1960s, Ocho Rios was the first coastal town chosen by the Jamaican government to develop specifically as a tourist resort. Today Ochi is defined by its cruise-ship stopover status -- several times a week during the Caribbean cruising season (November to March), several thousand passengers disembark and are shunted into minibuses to tour the local sites. It's best perhaps to plan trips at the weekends, when cruise ships rarely come to town.

Although its streets are invariably crowded, Ocho Rios is the most compact of all Jamaica's resorts. It's possible to walk to many of its attractions and, unlike Kingston or even Negril, all the downtown action is minutes away from most of the hotels and the beach. The town has a certain infectious energy and there are dozens of places in which you can eat and drink to your heart's desire. Shoppers will find several craft markets and numerous small malls selling duty-free goods. Island Village is one of Jamaica's most attractive shopping plazas – it even has its own small beach.

The surrounding countryside is a verdant swathe of green pastures and unspoilt rural communities. There are more accessible tourist attractions close to Ocho Rios than anywhere else on the island. Along the coast east of the town are some of the island's most luxurious all-inclusive hotel resorts. The new North Coast Highway brings Montego Bay – and, crucially, the airport – ever closer.

JTB (JAMAICA TOURIST BOARD)
📍 c/o TPDCO Ocean Village Plaza, Main St ☎ 974 7705
🌐 www.visitjamaica.com, www.tpdco.org ⏰ 09.00–17.00 Mon–Fri, closed Sat & Sun

BEACHES

Mahogany Beach

At the eastern end of Ocho Rios, where Main Street turns into the A3 or North Coast Highway, Mahogany Beach is a peaceful sandy cove backed by manicured lawns. An older, smarter crowd hangs out here and the atmosphere is almost genteel. There are watersports facilities and a very good beach bar and grill. Popular weekend barbecues and occasional live music events also take place on the beach.

ⓐ Main St, just past the Hibiscus Lodge Hotel ❶ 974 0833

Turtle Beach

Also known as Mallards or, more accurately, Ocho Rios Bay, the main town beach is a gently curving sweep of white sand hidden from view by the hotels that back onto it. Well-maintained facilities include showers, changing rooms, and several bars and snack kiosks. There is a long-established watersports operator that offers scuba diving and snorkelling trips.

ⓐ Main St, accessible from the Ocean Village Plaza ❶ 974 2853
🕐 08.30–18.00 daily ❶ Admission charge

THINGS TO SEE & DO

Dolphin Cove

Close to Dunn's River Falls is Dolphin Cove, the home of a number of stray bottlenose dolphins who are kept in a fenced-off section of the bay. There is the opportunity to stroke the mammals and swim with them; it

JAZZ FESTIVAL

The Ocho Rios International Jazz Festival is an annual music event held in venues in and around Ocho Rios, which attracts well-known singers of the genre.

❶ 927 3544 Ⓦ www.jamaicaculture.org/jazz

is all recorded on video, ready for you to purchase when you leave. It's an undeniably slick operation and immensely popular – booking at least a week in advance is essential. The site also has a nature trail through the woods with macaws, snakes and monkeys.

ⓐ A3 coast road westwards ☎ 974 5335
ⓦ www.dolphincovejamaica.com
🕒 08.30–17.30 daily ❗ Admission charge. Advance booking essential

Dunn's River Falls

Jamaica's premier tourist attraction is about 3 km (2 miles) from Ochi's town centre. Although permanently swarming with tourists as well as Jamaican families, the famous climb over rock ledges up the river while the waters of a 183-m (600-ft) waterfall gush down in cooling jets is really exhilarating. It takes about an hour to reach the top – most people follow a guide who exhorts everyone to hold hands (to prevent stumbling). At the river's mouth is a small white-sand cove with crystal-clear water that is far more attractive than the main town beach. Full facilities are on-site as well as an array of crafts for sale.

ⓐ A3 coast road westwards ☎ 974 2857 ⓦ www.dunnsriverfallsja.com
🕒 08.30–17.00 daily ❗ Admission charge

Reggae Xplosion, Island Village

Reggae Xplosion is the only museum in Jamaica to chart the fascinating and exciting history of Jamaican music, perhaps the island's finest export. The walls are covered with evocative photographs, there are music and video clips on hand to listen to and watch, and there's even a reconstruction of genius record producer Lee 'Scratch' Perry's recording studio.

ⓐ Junction of Main St and DaCosta Drive ☎ 675 8995
ⓦ www.islandvillageja.com 🕒 09.00–17.00 daily ❗ Admission charge

Shaw Park Botanical Gardens

Shaw Park was once the site of a fancy hotel. Now its 10 hectares (25 acres) of beautifully planted gardens high above the town are visited

⬆ *The sparkling blue waters of Ocho Rios*

by plant lovers and those seeking a little respite from the crowds downtown. A huge banyan tree is the highlight of the gardens, though there are many other unusual and impressive flowers and shrubs. The knowledgeable gardeners will point them out to you.

ⓐ Shaw Park Rd ⓣ 974 2723 ⓦ www.shawparkgardens.com
ⓛ 08.00–17.00 daily ⓘ Admission charge

CINEMA

There is one cinema in Ocho Rios:
Cove Theatre ⓐ Island Village ⓣ 675 8995

TAKING A BREAK

Bars & restaurants
Mr Humphrey's Pizza Café £ ❶   Tasty pizza slices and sandwiches.
ⓐ Main St ⓣ 974 8319 ⓛ 10.00–22.00 Mon–Sat, closed Sun

Ocho Rios Village Jerk Centre £ ❷   Popular local jerk venue with outdoor dining and lots of atmosphere. ⓐ DaCosta Drive ⓣ 974 2549 ⓛ 12.00–23.00 daily

The Healthy Way £ ❸   Vegetarian takeaway with a range of salads, stews and soups. ⓐ Ocean Village Plaza ⓛ 10.30–17.00 Mon–Sat, closed Sun

Mama Marley's ££ ❹   Decent Jamaican food, burgers and sandwiches inspired by Bob Marley's mother's home cooking. There's Bob Marley memorabilia and a gift shop on-site. ⓐ 52 Main St ⓣ 974 0197 ⓛ 10.00–22.00 daily

AFTER DARK

Restaurants
Bibibips ££ ❺   Standard Jamaican dishes presented with flair and

◓ *Cool waters at the Shaw Park Botanical Gardens*

imagination as well as American favourites. Good cocktails and a seafront setting. **ⓐ** 93 Main St **ⓣ** 974 8759 **ⓛ** 12.00–24.00 daily

Passage to India ££ ⑥ Standard Indian fare well cooked and presented in elegant surroundings. **ⓐ** Soni's Plaza, 50 Main St **ⓣ** 795 3182 **ⓛ** 12.00–22.00 daily

Evita's £££ ⑦ Long-standing Italian restaurant with classic and innovative pasta dishes. **ⓐ** Eden Bower Rd **ⓣ** 974 2333 **ⓛ** 12.00–15.00 & 18.00–23.00 daily

Toscanini £££ ⑧ One of the best restaurants on the island with classy Italian food of all kinds and a good wine list. The setting, on the terrace of a small plantation house, is very pretty. **ⓐ** Harmony Hall, Tower Isle **ⓣ** 975 4785 **ⓛ** 12.30–14.30 & 19.00–22.00 Tues–Sun, closed Mon

Nightlife
Glenn's Cocktail Bar ⑨ There is a very retro feel to this out-of-town cocktail bar with live jazz and a piano. **ⓐ** Tower Isle **ⓣ** 975 4360 **ⓛ** 17.30–23.00 daily

Jamaica'N Me Crazy ⑩ Disco in huge hotel that is patronised by tourists and open to non-guests. **ⓐ** Sunset Jamaica Grande **ⓣ** 974 2201 **ⓦ** www.sunsetjamaicagrande.com **ⓛ** 21.00–02.00 daily **ⓘ** Admission charge

Margaritaville ⑪ Like its bigger sister in Mo'Bay, Margaritaville is an all-singing, all-dancing bar and club with themed nights and a pool. **ⓐ** Island Village **ⓣ** 675 8800 **ⓦ** www.margaritavillecaribbean.com **ⓛ** 10.30–03.00 daily

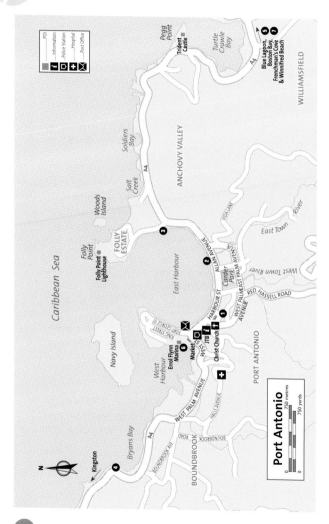

Port Antonio

Port Antonio (known as Portie) is the capital of lush, green Portland on the eastern coast of Jamaica and, with its twin harbours, has one of the loveliest settings anywhere on the island. Once it was the playground of the rich and famous – notably Errol Flynn, who loved the place. Before that, though, Port Antonio was known as a major banana port, inspiring the calypso song 'Day-O': 'Work all night for a drink of rum, daylight come and me wanna go home.' Even today, bananas bound for Europe and the US are loaded onto ships in the town's industrial wharf.

Flynn and his friends created an upmarket tourist industry here; the remnants of this, a series of elegant hotels, still exist. Nowadays, though, it is adventurous types who love Portie's off-the-beaten-track charm, and there is a plethora of small and interesting guesthouses in the area. Not a single all-inclusive hotel has breached the battlements of independent tourism here – yet. Instead, Port Antonio is a small gem in Jamaica, a laid-back place of beguiling charm.

BEACHES

Blue Lagoon
Not a beach, but on the coast, the Blue Lagoon is a famous bathing spot. The round turquoise pool is so perfectly shaped it's hard to believe it's natural; several films (most notably *The Blue Lagoon*) have been shot here. These days there are no facilities at the lagoon – the restaurant and watersports concessions have closed down – but anyone can come for a swim in the lagoon's clear, deep waters. Ignore anyone who tries to charge you an entrance fee.
ⓐ A4 coast road ⓒ No set hours

> ### JTB (JAMAICA TOURIST BOARD)
> ⓐ City Centre Plaza, Harbour St ⓣ 993 3051
> ⓦ www.visitjamaica.com ⓒ 08.30–16.30 Mon–Fri, closed Sat & Sun

Boston Bay

While most people head to Boston Bay for the jerk pork (see box on page 35), its small beach is known among Jamaicans for one thing only – surfing. The waves here are among the best in Jamaica and several of the local boys have become semi-pro. Boards can be rented from a shack on the beach and there's a simple lunchtime diner.

ⓐ Boston, A4 coast road ⓛ No set hours

Frenchman's Cove

Considered by many to be the most beautiful beach in Jamaica, Frenchman's Cove is pictured frequently in photos of the island. The private property of a once-grand hotel that barely functions these days, the beach is a gently curving stretch of fine white sand with a river running into it. Loungers can be rented and there's a small bar.

⬤ *Cream of the crop: Frenchman's Cove*

🄰 A4 coast road opposite San San Golf Course 🕿 993 7270
🔵 www.frenchmans-cove-resort.com 🕒 09.00–17.00 daily
🄸 Admission charge

Winnifred Beach

Winnifred Beach is one of the last really pretty public beaches in Jamaica. There is an excellent restaurant at one end, and a series of small drinks kiosks and horse rides for the children.

🄰 Fairy Hill, A4 coast road 🕒 No set hours

THINGS TO SEE & DO

Christ Church

A large red-brick Romanesque-style building, Christ Church is impressive enough to warrant a peek inside. The eagle lectern was donated by Captain Dow Baker, who made his fortune from Portland bananas.

🄰 Corner of Harbour St and West Palm Ave

Errol Flynn Marina

Most of the waterfront in Port Antonio is now part of the fancy marina. There are several smart restaurants, an attractive garden and even a small swimming pool. At one end is Folly Beach, once the town's public beach and now cleaned up for boat-hands and tourists alike. The area's only scuba-diving operator, Lady G'Diver, is also based here.

🄰 West Harbour 🕿 715 6044 🔵 www.errolflynnmarina.com

Lady G'Diver 🕿 715 5957 🔵 www.ladygdiver.com

Folly Point Lighthouse

North of the town is a small peninsula with a cricket ground and the remains of what was once one of the grandest houses in Jamaica, built in 1902 for an American banker: all that stands now is its pillars and staircase. The lighthouse is situated in an attractive flower garden and its keeper will let you wander round.

TAKING A BREAK

Cafés & restaurants

Dixon's Food Shop £ ❶ Fantastic vegetarian takeaway with a few tables upstairs. Salads and tofu reign. ⓐ Bridge St ❶ 993 3840 ❶ 11.30–23.00 daily

Oliver's Survival Beach £ ❷ Delicious fresh fish and Ital vegetable stew are served at this simple waterfront venue. ⓐ Allan Ave ❶ 384 4730 ❶ 12.00–21.00 daily

🔺 *Tending nets at Blue Lagoon*

AFTER DARK

Anna Banana ££ ❸ Tasty club sandwiches, Jamaican standards and seafood platters in a buzzing atmosphere. Occasional live music and karaoke sessions. ⓐ 7 Folly Rd ❶ 715 6533 ❶ 08.00–23.00 daily

Dickie's Best-Kept Secret ££ ❹ One of Jamaica's most extraordinary experiences is a lavish five-course meal in a tiny bohemian dining room under a roadside banana stall! Booking in advance is essential. ⓐ A4, just north of Port Antonio ❶ 809 6276 ❶ By appointment only

Woody's ££ ❺ Supremely friendly burger bar that has veggie options and fairy-lit décor. It's great for an early evening drink too. ⓐ Drapers, A4 coast road ❶ 993 7888 ❶ 12.00–21.00 daily

Norma's at the Marina £££ ❻ A branch of chef Norma Shirley's restaurant empire, this is a less formal version than Norma's at the Wharf House near Montego Bay. Located on the beach at fancy Errol Flynn Marina, it serves up imaginative, nouvelle Caribbean cooking. ⓐ Errol Flynn Marina ❶ 993 9510 ❶ 12.00–22.00 daily

San San Tropez £££ ❼ Italian place run by foody Italians with delicious thin-crust pizza, pasta and a great wine list. ⓐ San San Bay, A4 coast road ❶ 993 7213 ❶ 12.00–22.00 daily

BOSTON JERK PORK

At Boston Bay, jerk pork stalls line a lane off the main road – here the business of preparing the spiced meat is taken seriously and the barbecues, made with pimiento wood, are lit at first light. People come from several kilometres around to taste the best jerk pork in Jamaica.

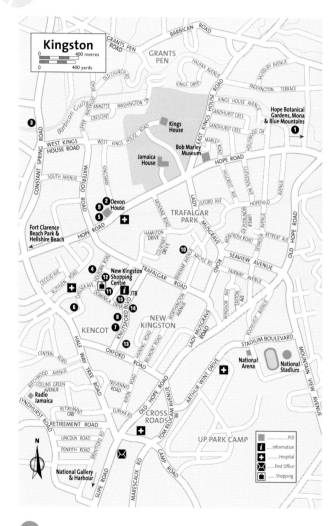

Kingston

Bad, bad Kingston Town. Jamaica's capital city has an appalling reputation. Gun-toting gangsters, no-go ghetto areas and rampant crime are all common images of the city. Although there is some truth in the clichés – the ghettos of West Kingston (Jones Town, Trench Town, Tivoli Gardens) are places where visitors should never venture after dark (and caution is also advised in the daytime) – in general travellers will be amazed at the city they find. A large percentage of Jamaica's population lives in Kingston and it's a cosmopolitan place with a thriving arts scene involving painting, music, dance and theatre. The University of the West Indies' (UWI) main campus, Mona, is also in Kingston.

Kingston was originally a modest village based around pig-rearing. When Port Royal – the centre of maritime trading across the bay – was devastated in the 1692 earthquake, its citizens moved over to Kingston and the city grew rapidly. By the early 18th century it had become a major port, shipping goods and slaves to the Spanish colonies of Latin America, and inhabited by wealthy merchants and traders. In 1872 Kingston succeeded in its bid to become Jamaica's capital city, taking the title from nearby Spanish Town.

Downtown Kingston runs out at the harbour, one of the world's biggest and an enduring part of Kingston's economy. The waterfront is a peaceful place, where locals shoot the breeze, take a stroll or fish from piers. The streets were once lined with grand 18th-century mansions, but many were destroyed in the 1907 earthquake and those that remain are in a dilapidated state. Strangely, their decay lends great atmosphere to an area that was once one of the wealthiest in the Caribbean. Here is the National Gallery of Jamaica and an impressive statue ('Negro Aroused') by renowned sculptor Edna Manley. Away from the harbour is Kingston's

JTB (JAMAICA TOURIST BOARD)
ⓐ 64 Knutsford Blvd ⓣ 929 9200 ⓦ www.visitjamaica.com
ⓛ 09.00–16.30 Mon–Fri, closed Sat & Sun

huge, sprawling Coronation Market and several attractive colonial buildings.

Midtown is called New Kingston and this is where the city's business is done. The leafy streets are lined with skyscrapers and have a plethora of hotels with all mod cons and excellent conference facilities. There are dozens of restaurants and bars of all kinds. The locals are too busy going about their working day to care about tourists, so hustling here is virtually non-existent. The area is dissected by Hope Road, where, conveniently, several of Kingston's most popular attractions are located.

Uptown Kingston is a series of lovely suburbs – Jack's Hill, Cherry Gardens – where Jamaica's wealthiest citizens live. Looming over the entire city are the Blue Mountains, the highest range in the Caribbean, which give the city skyline a kind of majesty and provide a much-needed breather from chaotic Kingston life.

BEACHES

Kingston proper has no beach – the waterfront is entirely taken up by the huge natural harbour. Still, there are several good beaches close by that are popular at the weekends with Kingstonians relieved to escape the city heat.

Fort Clarence Beach Park

Owned and run by the government's UDC (Urban Development Corporation), Fort Clarence is a lovely stretch of sand with changing and lifeguard facilities. There's a small snack-shop and regular live music events are held at the weekends.

ⓐ Hellshire Hills ⓣ 922 8310 ⓦ www.udcja.com ⓛ 10.00–17.00 Mon–Fri, 08.00–19.00 Sat & Sun ⓘ Admission charge

Hellshire Beach

Several kilometres west of Kingston, Hellshire Beach is more famous for its fried-fish vendors than its white sand and calm waters. Weekends are packed with local families tucking into delicious freshly cooked lobster

◔ Learn about the legend at the Bob Marley Museum

and fish. Watersports operators also turn up at the weekends, and there are horse rides along the sand for children.

ⓐ Hellshire Hills ● No set hours

THINGS TO SEE & DO

Kingston's attractions are close together. There are several on the same road in New Kingston, Hope Road.

Bob Marley Museum

This attractive colonial building was the reggae superstar's home from 1975 until his death in 1981 and has been kept much as he left it. It's a place of pilgrimage for Marley's many fans, but, even if you're not one of them, the museum is a fascinating insight into the lives and times of a musical legend. There are interesting photographic and album collections on the walls, an exhibition of stage costumes and a re-creation of Wail 'n' Soul, the tiny Trench Town record shop that Marley ran for a while. A cinema – once Marley's Tuff Gong recording studio – shows documentary footage of various concerts and interviews with the great man. There's a good café on-site and a shop selling all kinds of Marley-bilia.

ⓐ 56 Hope Rd ❶ 927 9152 ⓦ www.bobmarley-foundation.com
● 09.00–17.00 Mon–Sat, closed Sun ❶ Admission charge

Cinemas

Kingston has a couple of decent cinemas:
Carib Cinema ⓐ Cross Roads ❶ 906 1090
Palace Cineplex ⓐ 106 Hope Rd ❶ 978 8286

Devon House

Devon House was built in 1881 by Jamaica's first black millionaire, George Stiebel, who made his fortune from gold mining in Venezuela. Now owned by the government, the elegant house is furnished with 18th-century European and Caribbean furniture and has a grand hall painted with palm trees and tropical birds. The former stables now house a small

◯ *Tranquillity and elegance at Devon House*

collection of shops and several very good restaurants. Kingstonians love to come here to have wedding photos taken or to have lunch in the tree-filled yard – there are excellent patty and ice-cream shops.

ⓐ 26 Hope Rd ⓣ 929 6602 ⓦ www.devonhousejamaica.com
ⓛ 09.00–17.00 Mon–Sat, closed Sun ⓘ Admission charge

Hope Botanical Gardens

Once a sugar plantation, Hope Botanical Gardens are a favourite Kingston spot to relax with a book, a picnic or friends, particularly at the weekends. Expansive lawns, a lily pond and a collection of unusual tropical plants are the gardens' attractions, and there is also a small zoo. Currently extensive restoration is under way that aims to bring the gardens back to their former glory.

ⓐ Old Hope Rd ⓣ 970 3505 ⓦ www.moa.gov.jm/gardens ⓛ Gardens 08.30–18.00 daily; zoo 10.00–17.00 daily ⓘ Admission charge

⬥ Hope Botanical Gardens are perfect for relaxation

National Gallery

The National Gallery houses an impressive collection of Jamaican art, with pieces from virtually every local artist of note. Edna Manley, wife and mother respectively of prime ministers Norman and Michael Manley, was a renowned sculptor; her work dominates the first rooms of the permanent exhibitions. The brooding paintings of barber John Dunkley and dozens of wooden carvings by Kapo, another acclaimed Jamaican artist, are among the gallery's other highlights. There are also international works of art, contemporary photographs and even pieces of Taino craftsmanship on display.

🅐 12 Ocean Blvd 🕐 922 1561 🌐 www.galleryjamaica.com 🕒 10.00–16.30 Tues–Thur, 10.00–16.00 Fri, 10.00–15.00 Sat, closed Sun
🅘 Admission charge

Theatres

There are two excellent theatres that host plays, pantomime and dance performances.

Little Theatre 🅐 4 Tom Redcam Ave 🕐 926 6129

Philip Sherlock Centre for Creative Arts 🅐 UWI Mona Campus, Kingston 7 🕐 927 1047

TAKING A BREAK

Most eateries are clustered around the streets of New Kingston, where most hotels are also situated.

Restaurants

Ashanti Oasis £ ❶ Fantastic vegetarian café in a perfect spot. Serves up soup, veggie burgers and soya ice cream. 🅐 Hope Botanical Gardens 🕐 No phone 🕒 12.00–19.00 daily

Brick Oven £ ❷ Possibly the best patties in Jamaica. The lobster version is a meal in itself. 🅐 Devon House, 26 Hope Rd 🕐 968 2153 🕒 08.30–18.00 daily

East £ ❸ Japanese noodle bar with excellent sushi and sashimi.
Lunchtime specials. ⓐ Shop 51, Marketplace Mall, 67 Constant Spring Rd
❶ 960 3962 ❶ 12.00–18.00 Mon–Fri, closed Sat & Sun

Akbar ££ ❹ The best Indian food in Kingston with a good-value
lunchtime buffet. ⓐ 11 Holborn Rd ❶ 926 3480 ❶ 12.00–23.00 Mon–Sat,
closed Sun

Grog Shoppe ££ ❺ Sophisticated Jamaican fusion cooking as well
as lighter salads, quiche and sandwiches. Excellent Sunday brunches
and night-time entertainment. ⓐ Devon House, 26 Hope Rd ❶ 929 7029
❶ 12.00–24.00 daily

AFTER DARK

Chelsea Jerk Centre £ ❻ Popular local eatery with good jerked meat –
chicken or pork. Simple décor. ⓐ 7 Chelsea Ave ❶ 926 6322
❶ 12.00–22.00 daily

Prendy's £ ❼ Hellshire fish shack comes to town with lobster, crab
and conch specialities. Expect queues. ⓐ Putt 'n' Play, 75 Knutsford Blvd
❶ 859 7926 ❶ 18.00–23.00 Wed, Fri & Sat, closed Sun–Tues & Thur

STAYING SAFE AFTER DARK IN KINGSTON

Kingston's nightlife is the most vibrant of anywhere in Jamaica.
Excellent restaurants, drinking joints and nightclubs burst with
energy and atmosphere. However, crime is a way of life in some
parts of the city, and you should take extra care after dark. The
usual precautions apply – take a taxi if you're unsure of your
bearings and keep your wits about you.

Habibi Latino £££ ❽ Popular fusion (Cuban/Lebanese) restaurant with friendly staff and lots of atmosphere. Ⓐ 61 Knutsford Blvd
❶ 926 2285 ❶ 11.00–23.00 daily

Norma's on the Terrace £££ ❾ Jamaica's most famous chef, Norma Shirley, presides over Kingston's most elegant restaurant. Imaginative nouvelle Caribbean cuisine. Ⓐ Devon House, 26 Hope Rd
❶ 968 5488 ❶ 12.00–23.00 Mon–Sat, closed Sun

Red Bones Blues Café £££ ❿ Stylish bar, restaurant and music venue – one of night-time Kingston's most alluring places. Food is upmarket Jamaican with a twist. Ⓐ 21 Braemar Ave ❶ 978 6091 ❶ 12.00–01.00 Mon–Sat, closed Sun

Bars
Cuddy'z ⓫ Popular sports bar with baseball, cricket and football action on numerous TVs. Ⓐ 25 Dominica Drive ❶ 920 8019 ❶ 12.00–24.00 daily

Indies ⓬ This bar occupies a central location and has a friendly atmosphere, karaoke nights and DJs at the weekend. Ⓐ 8 Holborn Rd
❶ 920 5913 ❶ 12.00–24.00 daily

Mingles ⓭ Upmarket hotel bar with barbecues, live jazz and Latin dance classes. Ⓐ Courtleigh Hotel, 85 Knutsford Blvd ❶ 929 9000
❶ 12.00–24.00 daily

Nightclubs
Asylum ⓮ This is Kingston's most celebrated nightclub: expect plenty of action and smartly dressed crowds. Ⓐ 69 Knutsford Blvd ❶ 906 1828
❶ 21.00–06.00 daily

Quad ⓯ Four-floor disco with jazz club, go-go dancers, retro sounds and all the rest. Ⓐ 20–22 Trinidad Terrace ❶ 754 7823
❶ 21.00–06.00 daily

South Coast

The South Coast does not refer to the whole south coast of the island, but usually to the south coast of St Elizabeth, a western parish known as Jamaica's 'breadbasket' because of its rich soil and abundant agricultural produce. Mandeville is also part of the South Coast. It's a hot, sleepy place, comprising a string of unspoilt fishing villages, strange cacti-strewn desert landscapes and small, unhurried towns, which gives a taste of how Jamaica was before the all-inclusive resorts moved in.

The region's capital is Black River, a town of somnolent charm. It was once a wealthy place, the first in Jamaica to have electricity. Exporting logwood was the town's big business; now Black River is known more for its Great Morass, a large wetland with mangrove swamps, crocodiles and lots of birds including egrets, herons and wild ducks.

Most visitors head south to Treasure Beach. Not one beach but several, Treasure Beach is the finest example of small-scale tourism in Jamaica – and possibly in the whole of the Caribbean. There are no golf courses, no manicured stretches of white sand, but it's one of the safest and friendliest places on the island, with a wide range of accommodation, some gorgeous villas and an array of places to eat and drink in.

Beyond Treasure Beach is a series of local beauty spots, scarcely visited by tourists but worth the effort nevertheless.

BEACHES

The beaches of the South Coast are much wilder than in other parts of Jamaica. Many have black sand and virtually no facilities – just a shack serving cold beer and fried fish.

Font Hill Beach Park

This is the only private beach on the South Coast. Owned by the PCJ (Petroleum Corporation of Jamaica ⓦ www.pcj.com), it's a popular local spot. Clean white sand and good snorkelling at an offshore reef are its main attractions – there is also a bar, lockers and picnic tables.

ⓐ A2 highway heading east to Black River ❶ 462 9011

🕐 09.00–17.00 Tues–Sun, closed Mon ❶ Admission charge

Frenchman's Bay

Situated in the middle of the strung-out community of Treasure Beach, Frenchman's Bay is a long stretch of black sand with rolling waves. Several kiosks serve up drinks and fried fish. Access is via a series of footpaths – ask anyone in the village to show you how to get there.

ⓐ Treasure Beach

Great Bay

The beach here is the most beautiful in the area, with lovely swimming coves and a surrounding wilderness of palms, cacti and wild birds. There are no 'beach facilities' – it's a natural paradise.

ⓐ Treasure Beach

THINGS TO SEE & DO

Black River Safari

The Black River, so called because peat sediment at its bottom makes the water appear brown-black, runs through the wetlands of the Great Morass, and the boat trip 13 km (8 miles) upriver is a nature-lover's delight. There are guaranteed sightings of large crocodiles, most of which have pet names given to them by the boat crews, as well as all kinds of birds – and the odd fisherman in his dugout canoe. It's a hypnotic couple of hours. At journey's end there's a snack stop, and those brave enough can even swim!

ⓐ Follow High St to the iron bridge over the river; boats leave from docks on either side. See box on page 48 for further details.

Lovers' Leap

Where the Santa Cruz Mountains run down to the sea, there is a sheer drop from the cliffs of 610 m (2,000 ft). Local legend has it that two lovers, both runaway slaves from a nearby plantation, came here and – vowing never to be separated – hurled themselves into the sea. Legend or not, it's a great place to view the sunset and there's·an on-site bar handily placed to take in the amazing views.

2 Signposted from Springfield, 11 km (7 miles) east of Treasure Beach **1** 959 6634 **1** 08.00–sunset daily

Milk River Spa

The hot mineral springs of Milk River were discovered in the 18th century and have long been housed in the basement of the Milk River Hotel and Spa. Return visitors swear by the curative powers of the waters, though they are highly radioactive! The spa is rather ramshackle and old-fashioned (don't expect fluffy robes and whale music), but it has an understated charm and entrance fees are very reasonable.

2 Coast Road 32 km (20 miles) east of Treasure Beach **1** 902 4657 **1** 08.30–18.00 daily **1** Admission charge (not for hotel guests)

BLACK RIVER SAFARI TOUR OPERATORS

Several tour operators offer boat rides down the river and there is no discernible difference between them. If you haven't booked in advance it's worth just turning up – there are often spare places and tours leave up to five times a day.

South Coast Safaris 2 1 Crane Rd **1** 965 2513
St Elizabeth River Safaris 2 Behind the Hendricks Building, High St
1 965 2374

If you're looking for something a little different, try contacting Lloyd Linton. A local ecologist, Lloyd's Irie Safari trips provide more scientific information than standard tours.
Irie Safaris 2 12 High St **1** 965 2466 **1** Tours by appointment

TAKING A BREAK

Bars & restaurants

M&D Bar £ Local café/grocery store with jerk chicken, pork and tasty conch soup. ⓐ Calabash Bay, Treasure Beach ⓛ 09.00–22.00 daily

Turns £ Ice-cream parlour with cheap snacks and lunches. Popular local hangout. ⓐ High St, Black River ⓣ 965 2685 ⓛ 10.30–18.00 Mon–Sat, closed Sun

Little Ochi ££ People come from as far away as Kingston for the famous cooked-to-order fish and lobster at Little Ochi. There are outdoor tables on the beach, some housed in fishing boats! ⓐ Alligator Pond, 16 km (10 miles) east of Treasure Beach ⓣ 965 4449 ⓛ 12.00–sunset daily

Pelican Bar ££ One of Jamaica's most unforgettable experiences is a fried fish lunch, washed down with cold beer, at this rickety offshore bar. You'll need to pay a boatman to get you here (see box below).

Sunrise Bakery ££ Famously good bakery with fresh hard-dough bread, cakes and sweet stuff. ⓐ High St, Black River ⓛ 08.30–16.00 Mon–Sat, closed Sun

TOURS FROM TREASURE BEACH

Treasure Beach is a long-established fishing community. Boat rides to deserted beaches or fishing spots, as well as the offshore Pelican Bar, are easily arranged with local fishermen – ask your hotel for those they recommend. **Treasure Tours** (ⓣ 965 0126 ⓦ treasuretours.info) is a small local company that has an interesting list of community-based tours.

◔ *Little Ochi serves the best fried fish on the beach*

AFTER DARK

Cloggy's on the Beach £ Tasty fried fish and conch soup in pretty location on the beach. Hosts occasional sound-system parties. ⓐ Crane Rd, Black River ① 634 2424 ⓛ 12.00–22.00 daily

Fisherman's Club £ Atmospheric local bar with all-night disco beats and live music. ⓐ Treasure Beach

Waterloo Guest House £ Creaky old hotel with atmospheric terrace bar. Friday night jams are popular. ⓐ 44 High St, Black River ① 965 2278 ⓛ 12.00–21.00 daily

Wild Onion £ Relaxed bar with pool tables, dance floor and easy mix of locals and visitors. ⓐ Frenchman's Bay, Treasure Beach ⓛ 12.00–24.00 daily

Jack Sprat ££ Informal beach restaurant with home-made pizza and fish dishes. Interior is designed to look like an old-style rum bar, complete with vintage jukebox. Poetry and film nights. ⓐ Calabash Bay, Treasure Beach ① 965 3583 ⓛ 12.00–24.00 daily

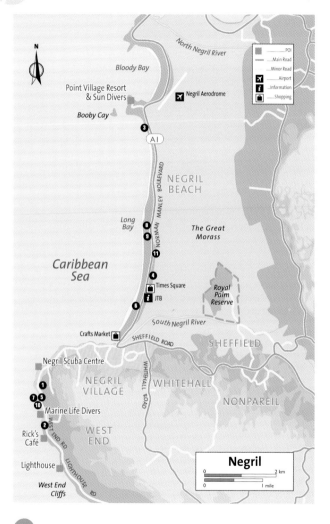

Negril

Negril sits at the westernmost point of Jamaica and was, until the 1960s, one of the island's remotest places. Its Spanish name, Punta de Negrilla ('black point'), refers to its isolation, which made it a perfect lair for pirates in the 18th century and for marijuana dealers years later. Then in 1959 a coast road was cut through the area known as the Great Morass – thousands of hectares of crocodile-infested swampland – and the many charms of Negril were finally 'discovered'.

It was foreign hippies who first came to Negril, drawn by its natural beauty and laid-back atmosphere, and their liberal influence lingers on. In Negril, anything goes – nude sunbathing, naked 'booze cruises', the consumption of ganja and other drugs including magic mushrooms, and all-night partying. When permissive resort Hedonism set up camp in the 1980s, with rumours of swinging, orgies and general debauchery, Negril's reputation was sealed. Even though the all-inclusive hotels have long moved in (to the northern fringes of town), there is a plethora of interesting guesthouses, boutique hotels and funky drinking joints in Negril, and its rock 'n' roll character remains.

Like Mo'Bay, the town is split into two distinctive parts. The 11-km (7-mile) beach, Long Bay, Negril's most famous attraction and one of the last in Jamaica to stay resolutely public, is backed by small hotels, beach bars and a road called Norman Manley Boulevard. It really is one of the loveliest stretches of sand in Jamaica, and the almost constant calmness of its pellucid water makes swimming a joy.

At its southern end the highway crosses the Negril River, then swings round and up to the West End, which is a meandering, potholed road high above cliffs that are riddled with caves. It's a sleepy place, devoid of shopping malls, hustlers and trouble. Here are some of Jamaica's

JAMAICA TOURIST BOARD (JTB)

ⓐ c/o TPDCO Times Square ☏ 957 9314 🌐 www.visitjamaica.com
🕐 09.00–17.00 Mon–Fri, closed Sat & Sun

classiest hotels, perched over the water – and here is where coachloads of tourists come to watch the sunset.

BEACHES

Although half the town doesn't actually have a beach, beaches are one of Negril's main draws. And, busy as they get, they're truly gorgeous: a Caribbean cliché of palm-fringed powder-fine sand and translucent turquoise waters.

Bloody Bay
At the northern end of Long Bay, beyond Rutland Point, the main beach becomes Bloody Bay; the name commemorates the butchering of whales that once took place on its shores. Once Negril's last area of undeveloped sand, the beautiful bay is now home to several all-inclusive resorts that have crudely fenced off their sections of the beach. Halfway along is the only remaining part of the bay open to the public. Approached through the woods between the sea and the main highway, the sand here is used by locals playing cricket, picnicking or sunbathing. There's a shack selling tasty fish and lobster cooked over an open fire.

Long Bay
Negril's main beach is still, blessedly, open to the public. Even though several major hurricanes in the last few years have diminished the width of the sand, it's still very long. There are half a dozen watersports

> **SPRING BREAK**
> Spring Break takes place in March and April. It's an annual booze-fest with live music and beach parties. It is actually laid on for holidaying American students, but anyone can attend. Contact the JTB for further details: ☎ 952 4425
> Ⓦ www.visitjamaica.com

operators offering every kind of service – glass-bottomed boat trips, jet-skiing, waterskiing, parasailing – and the beach is backed by a string of little bars, restaurants (some of them excellent) and craft stalls. Hustlers ply the sands selling hair-braiding and souvenirs. Entrance onto the beach is through a series of lanes running from Norman Manley Boulevard, and the action keeps going all night long.

THINGS TO SEE & DO

Negril's attractions really consist of the three s's – sun, sea and sand. That's during the day. The nights are claimed for serious partying. Many visitors never leave the beach.

Royal Palm Reserve

Situated in the heart of Negril's Great Morass, the reserve is a nature park dedicated to the protection of the royal palms that grow in this area, and has one of the largest collections of the stately tree. Rickety boardwalks lead a trail through the groves and well-informed guides explain and point out other plants and the surrounding ecosystem. It's an utterly peaceful place, a world away from the pleasure-seekers of Negril, and is a shamefully under-visited attraction. You may well be the only ones there.

ⓐ Springfield Rd ☎ 364 7407 🅦 www.royalpalmreserve.com
🕒 09.00–18.00 daily ❶ Admission charge. Dawn and dusk birdwatching is available with advance booking

Scuba diving and snorkelling

Negril has two long reefs running parallel to the West End Cliffs and several shorter ones along the beach; these offer the best scuba diving and snorkelling in Jamaica. Visibility is excellent, water temperature is warm year-round and, despite some environmental damage, the underwater world is vibrant and colourful. Things to see include several different kinds of coral, sea sponges, all manner of tropical fish, octopuses and the odd turtle. Highlights include the Throne Room, a large cavern with throne-shaped vegetation, Treasure Reef, with dozens of spotted moray eels, and a sunken ganja-smuggling plane, which missed its landing at Negril airstrip.

Sunset watching

This is an institution in Negril, which sits at the westernmost point of Jamaica and has the best vantage point anywhere on the island – some say that Negril's sunsets are the most beautiful in the world. As a flaming ball of orange sinks into the sea and the sky blazes streaky red then purple, dozens of tourists raise a large glass of potent rum punch to the wonders of Mother Nature. The most popular spot from which to see the sunset is Rick's Café, far along the West End Road. This cliff-top bar is an undoubtedly slick operation, providing live music and a long cocktail list – most people love it. Minibuses steam up the West End from Montego Bay and further afield before dusk falls. Local boys entertain the crowds by diving from the cliffs 12 m (40 ft) down into the sea. Foolhardy tourists can also have a go – jumping is safe; diving is trickier.

If you can't face the hordes at Rick's, several other places along the West End have sunset happy hours. The Rockhouse Hotel (see page 60) is actually located at the very western part of the West End.

Rick's Café ⓐ West End Rd ⓣ 957 0380 ⓦ www.rickscafejamaica.com ⓛ 17.00–22.00 daily

SCUBA-DIVING COURSES

There are a handful of excellent operators who all run PADI open water certification courses as well as one-day 'resort' courses for beginners:

Marine Life Divers ⓐ Samsara Hotel ⓣ 957 3245
ⓦ www.mldiversnegril.com

Negril Scuba Centre ⓐ Mariner's Beach Hotel ⓣ 957 4425
ⓦ www.negrilscuba.com

Sun Divers ⓐ Point Village ⓣ 474 7002 ⓦ www.sundiversnegril.com

TAKING A BREAK

Bars & restaurants

Choices £ ❶ Well-established restaurant serving tasty Jamaican cuisine. It is popular with both locals and tourists. ❷ West End Rd ❸ 957 4841 ❹ 10.00–19.00 daily

🔺 *Join the sunset crowd at Rick's Café*

◆ *Tropical heaven at Long Bay*

Original Rough House £ ❷ Healthy vegetarian and Ital dishes in a rootsy atmosphere. ⓐ West End Rd ☏ 957 0662 🕐 10.00–20.00 daily

Cosmos ££ ❸ Old favourite specialising in freshly cooked fish and lobster, located right on the beach. ⓐ Norman Manley Blvd ☏ 957 4330 🕐 12.00–21.00 daily

Selina's ££ ❹ All-day breakfast joint with delicious banana pancakes, freshly ground coffee and fruit salads. ⓐ Norman Manley Blvd ☏ 957 9519 🕐 09.00–20.00 daily

AFTER DARK

Three Dives £ ❺ Popular jerk joint with a nightly cliffside bonfire and annual jerk festival. ⓐ West End Rd ☏ 957 0845 🕐 17.00–24.00 daily

Angela's ££ ❻ Mid-range Italian restaurant with home-made pasta and thin-crust pizzas. ⓐ Norman Manley Blvd ☏ 957 9793 🕐 12.00–24.00 daily

Pirate's Cave ££ ❼ Perfect spot for sunset watching with good food (ribs, grilled chicken), great cocktails and a dartboard. ⓐ West End Rd ☏ 957 4410 🕐 12.00–23.00 daily

Le Vendome £££ ❽ Celebrated haute cuisine with classic French dishes – duck à l'orange, filet mignon – as well as food with a Caribbean flavour and weekly (every Thursday) live jazz sessions. ⓐ Charela Inn Hotel, Norman Manley Blvd ☏ 957 4277 🕐 12.00–22.00 daily

Ristorante da Gino £££ ❾ Top-notch Italian with a pretty terrace overlooking the beach. Particularly good for meat dishes, pasta and seafood. ⓐ Mariposa Hideaway Resort, Norman Manley Blvd ☏ 957 4918 🕐 12.00–24.00 daily

Rockhouse £££ ❿ One of Negril's finest restaurants is perched on the cliffs at the end of a romantic boardwalk. Jamaican fusion cuisine at its best. Booking essential in high season. ⓐ Rockhouse Hotel, West End Rd ① 957 4373 ② 09.00–23.00 daily

Nightlife

If you're looking for party action, Negril is your ideal destination. It's well known as one of the best places to see live reggae in Jamaica and there are frequent outdoor stage shows and big events. A long-standing tradition is to spend the evening dancing on the beach in front of Alfred's Ocean Palace, the Bourbon Beach Bar or Roots Bamboo, all of which have live bands several times a week. There is only one proper nightclub in Negril.

The Jungle ⓫ Large and impressive state-of-the-art club with slot machines and a sports bar as well as nightly DJs and dancing until dawn. 'Ladies' Night' on Thursdays is one of the most popular club nights in Jamaica – women get in free until midnight. ⓐ Norman Manley Blvd, opposite the beach ① 957 4005 ② 21.00–05.00 Thur–Tues, closed Wed ❶ Admission charge

● *Rafting on the Rio Grande River*

From Montego Bay

Montego Bay's long history as a prime tourist resort means that there are numerous tours well organised by tour operators from the city. It's easy to get away, and the small size of Jamaica means that many of the island's attractions are doable in day trips.

Cockpit Country

Cockpit Country lies in the interior of Trelawny and (to a much lesser extent) St James parishes and is the remotest region of Jamaica. Five hundred square kilometres (194 sq miles) of conical hills, sinkholes and several hundred caves have been formed over thousands of years by the limestone terrain of Cockpit Country – one of the world's finest examples of what geologists refer to as karst topography. This is a beautiful place, a land of strange pointed peaks and dense foliage wreathed in morning mists.

The harsh landscape means that there are few roads running through Cockpit Country and only a handful of tiny communities. Setting off on your own is not advised – it's easy to get lost and the area is

TOUR OPERATORS IN MONTEGO BAY
Barrett Adventures 382 6384 www.barrettadventures.com
Caribic Vacations 1310 Providence Drive, Ironshore 953 9895
www.caribicvacations.com
Glamour Tours 2 Gloucester Ave 940 3277
www.glamourtoursdmc.com
No Problem Tours 38 Round Hill Drive, Hopewell 956 5516
www.noproblemtours.com
Tropical Tours Providence Drive, Ironshore 953 9100
www.tropicaltours-ja.com

riddled with hidden caves and sinkholes. Best to head for one of three centres in the region – Albert Town, Windsor and Accompong – which are all geared towards tourism and can help with organised tours and local guides.

THINGS TO SEE & DO

Accompong Maroon Festival

Accompong is a pretty village, surrounded by breathtaking countryside, and is famous for its annual festival, held on 6 January, which celebrates the culture of Maroons, or fearsome escaped slaves who made their home in the remote hills, resisted colonisation in several battles with the British and still retain autonomy over the area. The festival involves the ritual roasting of a suckling pig, a procession through the village with elders dressed in traditional camouflage gear (vines) and much drumming, dancing and feasting. There is a community centre in

◆ *Feeding the hummingbirds at Rocklands Bird Sanctuary*

Accompong with a museum and an organised rota of excellent local guides. The road to Accompong from Montego Bay is fairly tortuous – better to go with an organised tour. Sun Venture Tours is a recommended ecotourism company in Kingston that regularly runs trips to Accompong; pick-ups from Montego Bay and other resorts can be arranged.

Sun Venture Tours ⓐ 30 Balmoral Ave, Kingston ⓣ 960 6685 ⓦ www.sunventuretours.com

Caving

Cockpit Country is known worldwide for its network of caves and caverns, more than 250 in number. Quashie River Sink is one of the most impressive, with its vast central chamber, but reaching it involves an arduous scrabble down steep cliffs; if you're fit enough and interested, it's possible to take a guided tour with Cockpit Country Adventure Tours (see opposite). Another of the area's most spectacular caves is Windsor Cave, 3.2 km (2 miles) of assorted caverns and chambers. Local guides are always available to show you round. Better still, the cave entrance is opposite Windsor Great House, which is owned by an English scientist: you can stay the night here. On Wednesday nights, the Great House hosts a four-course dinner when guests can meet visiting scientists and learn about the local flora and fauna.

For further information contact the well-informed Jamaican Caves Organisation: ⓦ www.jamaicancaves.org

Windsor Great House ⓐ Windsor ⓣ 997 3832 ⓦ www.cockpitcountry.com

Rocklands Bird Sanctuary and Feeding Station Long-established bird sanctuary with over a hundred species that specialises in hummingbirds. Visitors can help feed the tiny, jewel-coloured birds that are tame enough to perch on human fingers.

ⓐ Signposted off the B8, 24 km (15 miles) southwest of Montego Bay ⓣ 952 2009 ⓛ 14.00–17.00 daily ⓘ Admission charge

Tours with STEA

Based in Albert Town in the southeast of the region, the Southern Trelawny Environmental Agency (STEA) is an excellent source of information and advice with its own specialist tour company, Cockpit Country Adventure Tours. There is also the opportunity to stay in simple accommodation with local families.

STEA/Cockpit Country Adventure Tours ⓐ 3 Grant's Office Complex, Albert Town ❶ 610 0818 Ⓦ www.stea.net

TAKING A BREAK

Bars & restaurants

There are few restaurants in Cockpit Country – most of these are simple local 'cookshops' serving up rice and peas with stewed chicken or goat.

Peyton Place Pub £ The best of several basic bars in Accompong to have a cold drink; there are also rooms should you wish to stay overnight. ⓐ Accompong

Falmouth

Genteel Falmouth is the capital of the north coast parish of Trelawny. Once an important and wealthy port, it's now a sleepy market town that boasts the largest collection of Georgian buildings in Jamaica. Many, alas, have now fallen into disrepair, though there are long-standing plans to restore them. Nevertheless, strolling through Falmouth's elegant streets is a pleasurable experience, particularly interesting for those who love local history, and some of the finest Georgian buildings – the porticoed post office, the old courthouse – are still in daily use. There are several interesting churches to visit, such as the restored Baptist Manse and the William Knibb Memorial Baptist Church. The unhurried pace of life here is a world away from the big resorts along Jamaica's north coast, and Falmouth's people are easy-going and friendly.

THINGS TO SEE & DO

Bend-down market

Every Wednesday, the quiet streets of Falmouth are taken over by a bustling street market, with goods laid out on the ground (hence the name 'bend-down'). The market's wares include local fruit and vegetables, cheap clothing, CDs and knick-knacks. Although not designed to appeal to tourists, it's atmospheric and great fun – if you want to buy anything, you'll need Jamaican dollars.

Luminous lagoon

Surely one of the natural wonders of the world, Oyster Bay lagoon at nearby Rock is full of micro-organisms that glow in the dark. The water turns a luminous green and, if you jump in to swim, your movements will leave silvery trails in the sea.

The only way to really witness this truly astonishing phenomenon is to take a night boat trip from the aptly named Glistening Waters Restaurant and Marina in Rock (❶ 954 3229).

CHUKKA CARIBBEAN

Originally based on a polo field near Ocho Rios, Chukka Caribbean is now the biggest and most professional adventure sports tour operator in Jamaica. It runs almost a dozen different tours on the island, from two bases, and will pick up customers from hotels all along the north coast. Choose from horse riding, cycling, Jeep safaris, ATV (all-terrain vehicle) treks and kayaking, among other activities. Booking in advance is advisable.

Chukka Caribbean Montego Bay ❸ Blue Hole, Sandy Bay, Hanover
❶ 953 5619

Chukka Caribbean Ocho Rios ❸ Chukka Cove Farm, St Ann's Bay
❶ 972 2506 ❼ www.chukkacaribbean.com

○ *Falmouth Swamp Safari*

Outameni Experience

This new attraction, just outside Falmouth, entertains visitors with a well-conceived walk-through theme park focusing on Jamaica's cultural history. The lives of Taino, African, British and other ancestors of modern Jamaicans are depicted with songs, dancing and dramatic set pieces. It's all a little cheesy, but the performers' energy is very catching.

ⓐ Opposite Starfish Trelawny Hotel, 7 km (5 miles) east of Falmouth
ⓣ 954 4035 ⓦ www.outameni.com ⓛ 09.30–15.00 daily ⓘ Admission charge.

Walking tour

Those with an interest in architecture should contact Falmouth Heritage Renewal, whose American director, Jim Parrent, takes visitors on wonderfully informative walking tours of the town. The organisation has restored a number of small wooden houses, probably built by emancipated slaves, and helps local youngsters to train as craftsmen.

Falmouth Heritage Renewal ⓐ 9 King St ⓣ 617 1060
ⓦ www.falmouthjamaica.org

TAKING A BREAK

Bars & restaurants

A & A Exquisite Restaurant £ Excellent local diner with tasty, filling lunch including a good selection of vegetarian food and natural fruit juice.
ⓐ Thorpe St, Falmouth

AFTER DARK

Glistening Waters ££ Decent menu in waterfront restaurant with standard international cuisine as well as Jamaican favourites. ⓐ Rock
ⓣ 954 3229

Time 'n' Place ££ Funky little beachside hotel with nightly bonfires and good Jamaican food as well as killer cocktails and key lime pie. ⓐ Rock
ⓣ 954 4371 ⓛ 12.00–24.00 daily

From Ocho Rios

Ocho Rios, at the centre of the north coast, is the best-placed city in Jamaica for taking a day trip or tour. Now little more than two hours' drive from Montego Bay (and the international airport), it is also relatively close to Kingston, with a main road that cuts straight across the island. Thousands of cruise-ship passengers disembarking weekly in search of shore activities mean that tour attractions are being developed here more rapidly than anywhere else in Jamaica.

Cranbrook Flower Forest

Cranbrook Flower Forest is the home of a charming pair of retired schoolteachers who have a great love for and knowledge of tropical plants. They have turned their own land into a wonderfully peaceful park with landscaped gardens, grassy lawns and a collection of rare orchids. Ghetto blasters – and raucous behaviour generally – are not allowed, which makes this one of the most tranquil and civilised spots on an otherwise noisy island. A fast-flowing river runs through the site and at its head is a deep pool, perfect for bathing and cooling off.

ⓐ Cranbrook is 29 km (18 miles) west of Ocho Rios, signposted off the main coast road ❶ 770 8071 Ⓦ www.cranbrookff.com ❻ 09.00–17.00 daily ❶ Admission charge

---

TOUR OPERATORS IN OCHO RIOS
Many of the Montego Bay tour operators organise trips from Ochi and there are two locally based companies:

Ocho Rios Tour ❶ 370 2186 Ⓦ www.ochoriostour.com
Tourwise ⓐ 103 Main St ❶ 974 2323 Ⓦ www.tourwiseltd.com

THINGS TO SEE & DO

Canopy Tour

The latest addition to the park is a canopy tour, run by nearby tour company Chukka Caribbean (☎ 972 2506 ⓦ www.chukkacaribbean.com – see box on page 66 for details), which speeds you through treetops to enable prime jungle viewing on an intricate series of cables 14 m (45 ft) above the ground.

⬥ *Cranbrook Flower Forest*

Riverhead Adventure Tour

Gardeners will take interested visitors for an informative walk through the grounds, which starts on the main lawn and passes under a canopy of bamboo trees to the riverhead and its natural swimming pool. Tropical flowers pointed out include heliconias, birds of paradise, red euphorbia and bromeliads.

TAKING A BREAK

There is no restaurant at Cranbrook. Most people bring their own picnics and make a day of it; there are barbecuing facilities in the gardens if you fancy a hot snack. There's also a modest snack shop, serving patties and cold drinks.

Bob Marley Centre & Mausoleum

Bob Marley's birthplace is situated at Nine Mile in the rolling green hills of the interior of St Ann, which is also where the reggae legend is buried. Nine Mile is located about 40 km (25 miles) inland from Runaway Bay on the north coast and the road is badly maintained and winding. Easier than driving yourself is signing up for a standard tour (see box on page 69 for operators) from Ocho Rios or, much more fun, the Zion Bus Line (see page 73).

THINGS TO SEE & DO

Bob Marley's Home & Mausoleum

As you approach the village, it's clear that this is no sleepy Jamaican backwater – any more. The modest wooden shack and yard where Bob Marley grew up are now a pilgrimage site, crowded with local Rastafarians and visitors anxious to learn more about the musician's life and times. The highlight of the tour round the property, which points out the 'meditation stone' immortalised in Marley's 'Talkin' Blues', is the mausoleum where his

● Bob Marley Mausoleum at Nine Mile

body now rests. A concrete chapel with stained-glass windows is filled inside with a bizarre collection of mementos, tributes, flowers and lit candles, which make for a strangely moving experience.

ⓐ Nine Mile, St Ann ⓣ 843 0498 ⓛ 09.00–17.00 daily ⓘ Admission charge

Marley celebrations
Nine Mile is the central location for island-wide celebrations of Marley's birthday on 6 February. Sometimes one of his own children performs and there are sound systems, DJs and reggae musicians crammed into the tiny village. Aficionados camp out or stay up all night, but there is a basic hotel opposite the Centre – contact the Bob Marley Foundation (ⓣ 927 9152; ⓦ www.bobmarley-foundation.com) for reservations.

Zion Bus Line
This is a brightly painted replica of a Jamaican country bus, complete with drivers in Marley khaki overalls and on-board video shows of the Wailers in concert. The bus is operated as a day trip by **Chukka Caribbean** (ⓦ www.chukkacaribbean.com; see box on page 66 for more details) and snacks, rum punch and lunch are provided.

TAKING A BREAK

The Centre has an on-site vegetarian restaurant. The bustling nearby market town of Brown's Town has numerous simple diners serving tasty Jamaican food.

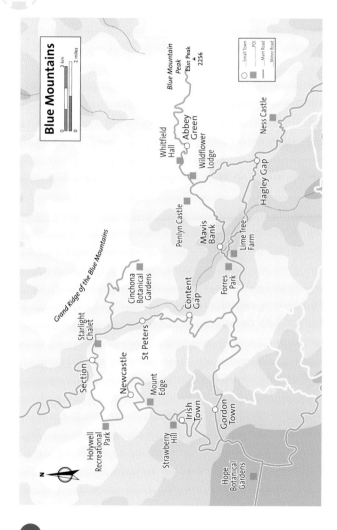

Blue Mountains

0 ___ 3 km
0 ___ 2 miles

Blue Mountain Peak
▲ East Peak
2256

Whitfield Hall
Abbey Green
Wildflower Lodge
Ness Castle
Hagley Gap

Penlyn Castle
Mavis Bank
Lime Tree Farm

Grand Ridge of the Blue Mountains

Cinchona Botanical Gardens
Content Gap
Forres Park

Starlight Chalet
St Peters

Section
Newcastle
Mount Edge
Irish Town
Gordon Town

Holywell Recreational Park
Strawberry Hill

Hope Botanical Gardens

○ Small Town
■ POI
—— Main Road
— Minor Road

N

74

From Kingston

Blue Mountains

Looming high above Kingston is the Blue Mountain Range, one of the longest continuous – and highest – mountain ranges in the Caribbean. Named on account of the smoky blue mists in which the mountains often seem to be wreathed, the Blue Mountains are staggeringly beautiful and have become, along with the adjoining John Crow Mountains (to the northeast), a designated national park and protected area.

Few people live here – it's still a rural place with tiny communities and terraced fields laced by tracks. The area is famed for its coffee, said to be the best in the world, and the small coffee plantations, with their rows of squat bushes with shiny green leaves, strung out over its slopes, are the only employers of any note.

The roads are frequently appallingly rutted – any exploration here by car requires a sturdy 4×4 – and many locals walk several kilometres to work or school each day. In spite of the hardship of their lives, mountain folk are warm-hearted and easy-going. Very little crime happens here, even though it's less than an hour's drive from the Blue Mountains' largest community, Mavis Bank, to Kingston.

TOUR OPERATORS IN KINGSTON

Kingston's attractions are mostly within its city centre. Those wishing to escape the noise and heat usually head for the hills – or, rather, the Blue Mountains. The north coast is also relatively close, with a main road running straight across the island from the capital to Ocho Rios.

Several tour operators take people sightseeing round the city and will also plan trips further afield.

Jamaica Story Tours 929 7895 www.uniquejamaica.com
Sun Venture Tours 30 Balmoral Drive 960 6685
www.sunventuretours.com

Many people visit the Blue Mountains to go hiking. This should not be attempted alone unless you are an experienced hiker – all the area's hotels (a selection of which are listed on page 78) can provide information about trails as well as good local guides.

THINGS TO SEE & DO

Blue Mountain Downhill Bicycle Tour

This exhilarating tour is a 30-km (18-mile) descent on two wheels from 1,700 m (5,600 ft) up in the mountains. A well-organised operation picks people up from their hotels in Ocho Rios and Kingston and, after a brief bike lesson and safety instructions, sends you off, whizzing past coffee bushes and tropical vegetation. As they say, it's downhill all the way, and pedalling is scarcely required. The end of the trip is marked with a refreshing dip in a lovely waterfall pool. Both brunch and lunch are included.

⬤ *Blue Mountain Peak is the highest point on the island*

Blue Mountain Bicycle Tours Ltd ③ 121 Main St, Ocho Rios ① 974 7075
ⓦ www.bmtoursja.com ⓒ Tours depart from Ocho Rios 08.00 (returning
17.30/18.00) Mon–Sat; or from Kingston 09.00 (returning around 17.00)
Mon–Sat

Hiking to Blue Mountain Peak

The most popular hike in the area is to Blue Mountain Peak (2,256 m/
7,402 ft), the highest point on the island. The standard way to go about
the climb is to start in the dark (01.00/02.00) so that, as you approach the
summit, dawn rises over Jamaica – on a clear day it's possible to see Cuba.
The 13-km (8-mile) trek takes between three and six hours and requires
reasonable levels of fitness; even though the route is signposted, it's a
very remote area and you should go with a good local guide. Most visitors
organise a trip to the top with their hotels, but there are also two simple
hostels (see below) at the start of the trail that provide guided tours,
dormitory accommodation and a hot meal on your return. The 'road' to
Abbey Green, where the hostels are located and the trek begins, is one of
the worst in Jamaica – ring ahead to organise a Land-Rover pick-up from
Mavis Bank.
Whitfield Hall ① 878 0514 ⓦ www.whitfieldhall.com
Wildflower Lodge ① 845 7202

Holywell Recreational Park

Holywell Recreational Park is a useful starting point for visitors to the Blue
Mountains. It's the official base station for mountain rangers, who can
provide detailed advice and information on trails and weather conditions
and, if they're informed of your movements, can keep an eye on your
progress and ensure that you don't get lost. It's also a lovely place in its
own right, an area of grassy pastures, woodland groves and simple hiking
trails – with fantastic views out over Kingston. You can rent cabins at
Holywell and there are two well-organised camping areas.

Holywell is managed by the JCDT (see box on page 78 for details). In
February the park hosts a day-long fair celebrating mountain culture,
with food stalls and music, called Misty Bliss – contact the JCDT.

TAKING A BREAK

Gap Café ££ Surprisingly chic restaurant with lovely garden terrace. Salads, sandwiches and cakes are all good. Steak and fish dishes also. ⓐ Hardwar Gap ❶ 997 3032 ⓛ 10.00–17.00 Tues–Sat, closed Sun & Mon

AFTER DARK

Strawberry Hill £££ Gourmet fusion food at one of Jamaica's best hotels. Staggering views over Kingston and a famous Sunday brunch. ⓐ Irish Town ❶ 944 8400 ⓛ 12.00–22.00 daily

ACCOMMODATION

Forres Park ⓐ Mavis Bank ❶ 927 8275 ⓦ www.forrespark.com
Lime Tree Farm ⓐ Lime Tree, just above Mavis Bank ❶ 881 8788
ⓦ www.limetreefarm.com
Mount Edge Guest House ⓐ Just south of Newcastle ❶ 944 8151
ⓦ www.mountedge.com
Starlight Chalet & Health Spa ⓐ Silver Hill Gap, near Section ❶ 969 3070
ⓦ www.starlightchalet.com
Strawberry Hill ⓐ Irish Town ❶ 944 8400 ⓦ www.islandoutpost.com

JCDT

The Jamaica Conservation and Development Trust (JCDT) manages the Blue Mountains National Park and is a good source of information on the area. They have an office in Kingston and their base in the Blue Mountains is at Holywell Recreational Park (see page 77). ⓐ 29 Dunbarton Ave, Kingston ❶ 960 2848
ⓦ www.greenjamaica.org.jm

Port Royal & Lime Cay

'The wickedest city on earth' was a pirates' haven in the late 17th century, full of roistering outlaws, loose women and drinking establishments. Little remains of the original town – it was devastated by an earthquake in 1692 and now lies beneath the sea – but Port Royal still has a potent seafaring atmosphere. Fort Charles houses an interesting museum, with artefacts from the town's heyday, and there are several semi-ruined buildings scattered around, including an ammunition store, a naval hospital and a jail. Nowadays the slightly forlorn place is proud of its fish restaurants, which are inexpensive and well patronised at the weekends.

Port Royal is reached by road – it's 15 minutes from downtown Kingston. ◎ City bus: no 98

THINGS TO SEE & DO

Boat trip to Lime Cay

A tiny uninhabited island in Kingston Bay, Lime Cay is a cliché – fine white sand with the odd palm tree. During the week it's deserted and you'll need to bring your own food and drink, but at the weekends it's a party place for Kingstonians and vendors sell snacks, jerk chicken and cold beers.

Lime Cay is reached by a 15-minute boat ride from Port Royal. Boats run regularly from the **Morgan's Harbour Hotel** (❶ 967 8040) and the **Y-Knot Bar** (❶ 967 8448).

Fort Charles

Fort Charles is the most impressive of Port Royal's original buildings and was once surrounded by water. Now it is approached by crossing a large parade ground and houses a small but fascinating Maritime Museum. The museum gives an overview of the history of Port Royal, as well as displaying treasures hauled from the water after the earthquake – such as cannonballs, tools and coins.

ⓐ Port Royal ❶ 967 8438 ● 09.00–17.00 daily ❶ Admission charge

St Peter's Church

Although the façade of St Peter's is relatively new, as is its roof, the interior has scarcely been changed since its construction in 1726. Features include an attractive carved organ loft, complete with English-made organ. The church holds a collection of silverware that is supposed to have been owned by the pirate Henry Morgan and has a small overgrown churchyard with ancient tombs. If the church is locked, locals will know who holds the key.

ⓐ Church St, Port Royal

TAKING A BREAK

Gloria's Rendezvous £ Most popular fish joint in town with tables on the street and tasty fish, shrimp and lobster. ⓐ 5 Queen St, Port Royal

Morgan's Harbour Hotel ££–£££ Elegant and historic hotel on the coast with two eateries – Red Jack with an outdoor bar for casual lunchtime meals and the upmarket Quartermain for excellent seafood.
ⓐ Waterfront, Port Royal ⓣ 967 8040 ⓦ www.morgansharbour.com

AFTER DARK

Y-Knot Bar ££ Atmospheric waterfront bar with dancing at the weekend and decent food.
ⓐ Waterfront, Port Royal ⓣ 967 8448

GREEN JAMAICA

Unique Jamaica is an ecotourism umbrella operation that brings together a range of tours and holiday packages specialising in exploring the natural beauty of Jamaica. Tours include trips to an organic farm, the Greencastle Estate in St Mary, and to the Elysium Forest Sanctuary in Lethe. ⓣ 929 7895 ⓦ www.uniquejamaica.com

Mandeville

Mandeville, situated mid-island towards the South Coast, is the only inland Jamaican town of noted importance – and one of the most prosperous. Founded in 1816 and named after Viscount Mandeville (son of the then Governor of Jamaica), its balmy location on the slopes of the Don Figuero Mountains has made it a long-time refuge for the wealthy from the heat of the coast. In Mandeville are Jamaica's first public library, its first golf club and one of its first hotels (which has an English-style pub).

Originally it was plantation owners and exhausted soldiers who came to holiday in Mandeville, drawn by its genteel atmosphere. Nowadays it's the province of returnees – retired Jamaicans returning from the UK and the US to spend the rest of their days in the cool climate of the hill town. The local bauxite industry – and its well-paid expat managers – has added to Mandeville's moneyed community. The streets are calm and safe; it's an elegant and peaceful place. The main square is an attractive spot, with several good Georgian buildings, among them the limestone courthouse. There's also a small, friendly market and several rather quaint shopping malls.

THINGS TO SEE & DO

Community tourism

Jamaican community tourism was really kick-started in Mandeville, the brainchild of local hotelier and human whirlwind Diana McIntyre-Pike. Her company, Countrystyle International, takes people on low-key tours that introduce visitors to Jamaicans and small rural communities. Most interests are catered for – you can meet local gardeners or musicians, go to a secondary school to see how Jamaican children are taught and even learn how to cook various popular dishes. If you're lucky – and she's not busy! – the inimitable Diana might take you out herself. The opportunity to stay in private Jamaican homes is also offered.

Countrystyle International 🅰 Astra Inn, 62 Ward Ave, Mandeville
🕓 488 7207 🆆 www.countrystylecommunitytourism.com

Huntingdon Summit

Rather out of keeping with the gentility of Mandeville, Huntingdon Summit is the kitsch mansion owned by the town's former mayor, eccentric millionaire Cecil Charlton, who made his fortune from betting shops. Octagonal in shape, the house is stuffed with glitzy 'antiques' and lavish furnishings. It also has a swimming pool with swim-up bar and a re-creation of the famous Bamboo Avenue (the real thing is situated on Jamaica's inland A2 highway) in the garden. ⓐ George's Valley Rd, May Day ⓣ 962 2274 ⓒ By appointment only

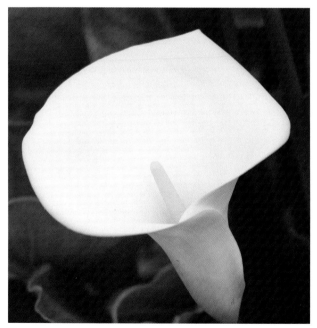

⬣ *Exquisite orchids grace Mrs Stephenson's Garden*

Mrs Stephenson's Garden

Carmen Stephenson is well known as a keen gardener in Mandeville and her lovely private garden is the headquarters of the venerated Manchester Horticultural Society. It is filled with anthuriums and orchids. Carmen will show you round herself if you call first to make an appointment.

ⓐ New Green Rd ❶ 962 2909 ⓛ Daylight hours ❶ Admission charge

TAKING A BREAK

Cafés & restaurants

Di Windies Grill £ Sports-themed lunch venue with good-value Jamaican dishes and burgers. ⓐ James Plaza ❶ 962 9463

Bird of Paradise ££ Popular new eatery with Jamaican, Italian and American dishes on extensive menu. Imaginative fusions of all three cuisines, served up elegantly and at very reasonable prices.
ⓐ 1 Brumalia Rd ❶ 962 6529 ⓦ www.birdofparadisejm.com

TAXI TOURS

With the high cost of car hire in Jamaica and the lack of public transport, an increasing number of tourists have taken to hiring a taxi driver for the day. Get your hotel or the tourist board to recommend reliable drivers or contact the local branch of JUTA (Jamaica Union of Travellers Association).

Kingston ❶ 927 4534
Montego Bay ❶ 952 0813
Negril ❶ 957 9197
Ocho Rios ❶ 974 2292

AFTER DARK

The New Den £ Diners in this rambling colonial house eat in what were once bedrooms. There is an extensive menu – meat and fish as well as sandwiches and pizza – and fun Friday-night jam sessions on the lawn. ⓐ 35 Caledonia Rd ❶ 962 3603 🕐 12.00–21.00 Mon–Sat, closed Sun

Mandeville Arms ££ English-style 'pub' with sedate atmosphere and late hours. ⓐ Mandeville Hotel, 4 Hotel St ❶ 962 9764 ⓦ www.mandevillehoteljamaica.com 🕐 16.00–23.00 daily

Bloomfield Great House £££ One of Jamaica's best purveyors of 'nouvelle Caribbean' cuisine. Tables are on the terrace of a restored Great House with a revolving art exhibition on the walls. There's an interesting wine list. ⓐ 8 Perth Rd ❶ 962 7130 🕐 18.00–22.00 daily

🔾 *A fishing boat at Negril beach*

Food & drink

Jamaican cuisine is a satisfying mix of well-spiced flavours and wholesome comfort food. As elsewhere in the Caribbean, and all over Latin America, rice and peas (actually small red beans) is an everyday staple, served with chicken or fish and side dishes of starchy vegetables. Seafood (lobster, crayfish, prawns) is plentiful and reasonably priced. The fiery Scotch bonnet pepper, one of the hottest, is used to give a kick to island food, which is usually washed down with cold beer, rum-based cocktails or natural juices.

MEAL TIMES

Breakfast

Traditionally, breakfast in Jamaica is ackee and salt fish. Ackee, a bland yellow fruit that looks like scrambled egg, is fried up with salt cod, tomatoes and sweet peppers. Rundown is smoked mackerel cooked with coconut milk and onions. Another Jamaican favourite is filling cornmeal, plantain or peanut porridge, which is laced with nutmeg. Tourist restaurants serve up fruit salads, eggs and bacon, and pancakes.

Lunch & supper

Lunch and supper consist of similar meals. These are usually chicken or fish served up with rice and peas, vegetables (mostly callaloo or pumpkin) and one or more kinds of starch (see page 94). A popular dish is brown stew, a glutinous, spicy sauce that is served with chicken or fish.

FAITH'S PEN

One of the most authentic, though far from scenic, eating experiences in Jamaica is the strip of roadside stalls at Faith's Pen on the busy Ocho Rios to Kingston highway. Blaring radios, truck drivers joshing, clouds of aromatic smoke and the most delicious Jamaican food imaginable at really low prices make eating at Faith's Pen a memorable occasion.

Escovitched fish is fish marinated in vinegar, hot peppers and thin strips of other vegetables and then fried. Cow foot (cow's feet stewed with butter beans and Scotch bonnet pepper) is not for those of a sensitive disposition. Many Jamaican workers have a box lunch, which simply means a packed lunch – the middle of the day sees any open-air space crowded with people enthusiastically tucking into the contents of white polystyrene containers.

BEVERAGES
Rum

Rum is the drink of choice in Jamaica. The variety most often drunk is Wray & Nephew's Overproof, a potent white rum that is mixed with fresh fruit to make rum punch or daiquiris. It also goes well with Ting (a grapefruit soda). Those looking for a smoother tipple should try Appleton's Special, a rich golden liquid which just needs ice – VX is an oak-aged reserve edition and even better. There are a number of rum liqueurs – the best is Tia Maria, which is coffee-flavoured.

APPLETON'S RUM ESTATE TOUR

The Wray & Nephew rum distillery at Appleton, in the south centre of the island, is the oldest in the English-speaking Caribbean. One of the most popular tourist attractions in Jamaica is an hour-long tour round the factory, with a chance to see how sugar cane is turned into the delicious drink. It is followed by informative tasting sessions.

The rum distillery is not easy to find. Most tour operators in Jamaica run trips to Appleton, which is set in stunning scenery and close to YS Falls.

ⓐ Appleton, near Maggotty, St Elizabeth ☎ 963 9215
ⓦ www.appletonrumtour.com ⏰ 09.00–16.00 daily
ⓘ Admission charge

Beer

Nothing accompanies spicy Jamaican food and hot sunshine better than a cold beer. The most popular and tasty brand is Red Stripe, which comes in stubby brown bottles. Imported lager is widely available too – particularly Heineken. Jamaicans also drink bottled Guinness® and other kinds of stout, usually served 'hot' (not chilled).

Non-alcoholic beverages

Fresh fruit juice is very refreshing – June plum, guava and soursop are popular. Also refreshing are ice-cold jellies, coconut water served up in the fruit itself and commonplace on the coast. Sky-juice consists of shavings of ice drizzled with fruit syrup. Home-made ginger beer is often found in local cookshops and is delicious, though very strong. At Christmas time, sorrel juice, a bright red drink made from hibiscus flowers, is traditional.

The most famous non-alcoholic drink in Jamaica is coffee (though Jamaicans themselves rarely drink it). The Blue Mountain variety is considered to be among the best coffee in the world and 90 per cent is exported immediately to Japan.

FRUIT & VEGETABLES

The tropical climate of Jamaica means that anything grows. Root vegetables – such as pumpkin, squash, yam and carrots – appear on menus more than salad ingredients. There is a wide variety of exotic

COFFEE FACTORY TOURS

The main Blue Mountain processing plant, Jablum Jamaica Ltd, is based in Mavis Bank and offers interesting factory tours. It's possible to see how hands-on the whole business still is: the beans are sorted manually and laid out to dry in the factory yard before being roasted. You will also have an opportunity to taste the excellent brew and buy it at very reasonable rates. ⓐ Mavis Bank, Blue Mountains ⓣ 977 8528 ⓦ www.jablumonline.com
ⓛ 09.00–15.00 Mon–Thur, closed Fri–Sun ⓘ Admission charge

fruit, naturally. Look out for the humble banana – Jamaican bananas are among the tastiest in the world.

Exotic vegetables

Callaloo is a leafy green vegetable, similar to spinach and served steamed with onions. Cho-cho is pale green and avocado-shaped with a delicate flavour. Okra is thin and pointed with a glutinous texture, and is often added to Ital stews.

FACTORY TOURS

The best-known brand of hot (chilli) sauce, a bottle of which sits on even the smartest restaurant tables in Jamaica, offers small but charming tours round its factory premises so that visitors can see how the sauce is made. Although exact recipes are kept secret, its main ingredients are chilli peppers, tomatoes, onions, raisins, mangoes, tamarind and other spices. Visitors can watch its progress from the first stages, via bubbling vats of the precious red liquid and then to the final bottling process.

Pickapeppa Hot Sauce Factory ⓐ Shooters Hill, Williamsfield, near Mandeville ⓣ 603 3440 ⓦ www.pickapeppajamaica.com ⓛ 09.00–15.00 Mon–Thur, closed Fri–Sun ⓘ Admission charge

Another 'hot' product of Jamaica is Walkerswood jerk seasoning, perfect for amateur chefs. Walkerswood began life 80 years ago as a community project in a pretty rural village and is now exported all over the world. Its factory tour shows visitors how jerk marinades are made, how to cook jerked meat and how local herbs and spices are grown and used.

Walkerswood Jerk Country Tour ⓐ Walker's Wood, near Ocho Rios ⓣ 917 2318 ⓛ Tours by appointment ⓘ Admission charge

Jamaica's juiciest and best produce is readily available

Exotic fruit

Ortanique is a Jamaican-bred combination of orange and tangerine. Otaheite apples are bright red and pear-shaped with crisp white flesh. Soursops are large custard apples, often made into delicious juice.

INTERNATIONAL FARE

Jamaica's long-standing status as a major tourist resort means that, when it comes to food, all tastes are catered for. The big three resorts (Montego Bay, Negril and Ocho Rios) have branches of US fast-food chains – Burger King, KFC and McDonald's – as does Kingston. These places also have a variety of restaurants serving international cuisine, including French, Chinese, Italian and Indian. The all-inclusive hotel chains, which usually have several restaurants on-site, tend to serve up this type of food rather than Jamaican home cooking. If you or your children prefer to stick to familiar dishes such as fish and chips or pizza, you won't go hungry.

SNACKS

The most ubiquitous Jamaican snack is the patty, a flaky pastry case generally stuffed with spiced beef or chicken. Other flavours include callaloo (a type of spinach) and lobster. There are two recommended chains of patty shops, Tastee and Juici Beef, and each town has its own local place – the most popular have lunchtime queues. Devon House in Kingston has an excellent patty shop, and there's a small bakery, Lucky Tree Pastry, in Savanna-la-Mar on the South Coast, which is famed for its vegetable patties. Jamaicans also snack on bun and cheese, a

> **WHICH WAY TO PAY?**
> While all tourist restaurants in Jamaica take US dollars and debit/credit cards, most of the smaller 'cookshops' (often hole-in-the-wall cafés) that serve up local specialities only accept Jamaican currency in cash. If you want to try out roadside island food you'll need to carry some Jamaican dollars.

sweet bun sold with a lump of hard yellow cheese that is not terribly appetising. Otherwise listen out for peanut sellers in downtown areas – the high-pitched whistle of the pushcart announces the arrival of the 'nuts man'.

Those with a sweet tooth will find all sorts of goodies in local bakeries, including bullas (flat, heavy ginger cakes), gizzadas (small tarts filled with shredded coconut and cinnamon) and coco bread. More unusual these days is duckanoo, a heavy African pudding made from sweetened and steamed cornmeal that is traditionally served in a banana leaf.

SPECIALITIES

Jerk chicken & pork

The most famous of all Jamaican foodstuffs is fiery jerk chicken and, more authentically, jerk pork. Jerked meat is centuries old and was developed by runaway slaves who hunted wild pigs and then preserved their flesh with a blend of local spices including pimiento (also known as allspice). All over the island, roadside vendors wheel oil-drum barbecues out at night and roast slabs of chicken (marinated in spicy jerk sauce) over hot coals. Jerk chicken is served in foil with a slice of hard-dough bread (very dense and slightly sweet). Less ubiquitous is jerk pork, though a series of open-air eateries in Boston Bay in Portland still cook traditionally over shallow pits of pimiento wood – this is renowned as the best jerk pork on the island. Several specialist chains also serve up a range of jerked meat; the best of these is Scotchies.

Soup

Hungry Jamaicans often stop for a cup of soup from the roadside. There are several kinds: pepperpot, which is a thick vegetable and meat mix; fish tea, which is made from steamed fish and vegetables; and conch soup, a spicy broth made from the small snail-like sea creature.

Goat

Goats run all over the island. Not surprisingly, they feature on menus. Curried goat is a popular lunchtime dish. Less well known is mannish

◆ *Jerk chicken vendors can be found all over the island*

water, a strong blend that includes the head, testicles and feet of a goat. This is made into a hearty soup, known for its aphrodisiac qualities and traditionally drunk by bridegrooms on the eve of their wedding. Spur Tree Hill near Mandeville is the best place to eat goat.

Ital food

Ital (vital) food is an intrinsic part of Rastafarianism. Vegetarian, and with no salt used, most dishes are a mixture of seasoned soya protein, tofu or gluten stewed with vegetables. Ital restaurants are usually simple cafés, often marked out by Rasta colours (red, green and gold).

STARCH

Starchy foods are part of every meal in Jamaica – many plates come laden with at least two different varieties. These include cassava, yam, potatoes (known as 'Irish' to differentiate them from sweet potatoes) and plantains (boiled or fried). But there are also some more unusual types: bammy is a hard biscuit made from cassava flour, soaked and then fried or steamed – it's traditionally served with fried fish; breadfruit is large, spiky-skinned fruit that is best roasted overnight and then fried in wedges; dumplings come either boiled or fried; festival is a sausage-shaped savoury doughnut served with jerked meat.

Shopping

Every tourist resort in Jamaica has half a dozen souvenir shops selling t-shirts, tropical patterned bags and wraps, and Rasta-coloured tat. Lovers of kitsch will find themselves in heaven. Many of the larger hotels have a better selection of souvenirs in on-site boutiques. Alternatively, head for one of the designated craft markets in each town. These are usually well organised and it's always possible to bargain (called 'higgling' in Jamaica) with vendors.

IN-BOND SHOPPING

Jamaica has a thriving industry centred on in-bond or duty-free goods – mainly expensive watches, jewellery and perfume. Malls dedicated to selling these items can be found in all the resorts. Savings vary from 20 to 40 per cent and goods have to be purchased in US dollars or with a major credit card.

City Centre Mall, Fort St, Montego Bay
Soni's Plaza, Main St, Ocho Rios
Taj Mahal, Main St, Ocho Rios
Times Square, Norman Manley Blvd, Negril

ART

There is a fine tradition of talented artists working in Jamaica. Much of the work consists of naïve and colourful paintings and is rarely found outside the island. Kingston has a plethora of art galleries, but there are several well-established outlets at which to buy paintings and sculpture in other places too.

> **GCT**
> Jamaica has a General Consumption Tax of 16.5 per cent, which is added to all goods at point of sale.

Frame Centre
ⓐ 10 Tangerine Place, Kingston ⓣ 926 4644

Gallery of West Indian Art
ⓐ 11 Fairfield Rd, Catherine Hall, Montego Bay ⓣ 952 4547
ⓦ www.galleryofwestindianart.com

Harmony Hall
ⓐ Tower Isle, Ocho Rios ⓣ 974 2870 ⓦ www.harmonyhall.com

Mutual Gallery
ⓐ 2 Oxford Rd, Kingston ⓣ 929 4302

Revolutionary Gallery
ⓐ 52 Lady Musgrave Rd, Kingston ⓣ 946 0053

MARKETS

Every sizeable town in Jamaica has a market (usually in a covered building), selling fruit and vegetables as well as cheap clothing and household goods. These are highly atmospheric places, often crowded, with cheap cookshops for lunchtime fuel and good-natured banter between market traders. If you're planning to visit the big markets, you'll need your wits about you.

Craft Market, Montego Bay Possibly the best craft market on the island, with a wide array of different goods in attractive surroundings. There's also an excellent café here for lunch. ⓐ Harbour St, Montego Bay
ⓛ 08.30–early afternoon Mon–Sat, closed Sun

Half Moon Shopping Village, Montego Bay Part of the huge Half Moon Resort, this is a state-of-the-art mall with designer goods, in-bond shops and the Bob Marley Experience Shop, which boasts the largest collection of Marley-inspired t-shirts in the world. ⓐ Ironshore, Montego Bay
ⓛ 08.30–early afternoon Mon–Sat, closed Sun

Island Village, Ocho Rios Island Village is the shopping mall with everything – it even has a cinema, live music performances and its own beach. There's an excellent CD shop as well as the usual souvenir places.

Orange Street, Kingston Music lovers should head to Orange Street in downtown Kingston, which is lined with record shops, many of them attached to small recording studios. Old vinyl discs are available as well as the latest CDs.

△ *Island Village, Ocho Rios*

🔊 *Woodcarvings are popular in Jamaica*

SOUVENIRS
Coffee

Blue Mountain coffee is much cheaper in Jamaica than elsewhere. Look for the hessian bags and blue label of Jablum (Ⓦ www.jablumonline.com), which processes some of the most superior beans. Old Tavern Estate coffee, which comes from a small family-run farm in the Blue Mountains, is possibly the best in the world and is available in upmarket outlets.

Rum

One of the best souvenirs to purchase in Jamaica is rum, which is much cheaper on the island than anywhere at home. As well as the standard fare, there are several kinds of oak-aged Appleton's rum that are not only delicious but also exceptional value. These can be bought all over the island – the best bargains are found in large supermarkets. The Jamaica Farewell shops in Montego Bay and Kingston airports package bottles in handy cardboard carrying cases for no extra charge. Visitors returning to the EU should note that they can only take home 1 litre of spirits.

Woodcarvings

Jamaica does a roaring trade in African-style woodcarvings. Many of these are now garishly painted and factory produced. If you're interested in the real thing, ask your hotel for recommendations and seek out craftsmen who have workshops where you can watch the carving in progress. Alternatively, head for one of the art galleries (see page 95), though prices will be higher there.

ILLEGAL PURCHASES

Both black coral and tortoiseshell products are widely touted for sale, but be warned – the trade in these endangered species is illegal and you could be liable to hefty fines if caught buying them. Also avoid buying pretty conch shells. While they can be legally purchased, their popularity has led to the large-scale diminution of conch in Jamaican waters.

Children

Jamaicans love children, and the island's informality means they are welcome in all but the smartest restaurants. Many of the island's attractions are suitable for children and most of the large resort hotels have organised childcare facilities and special activities laid on.

ACTIVITY & WATER PARKS

Kool Runnings One of Negril's most popular attractions is a water park with seven huge slides – the largest is 106 m (350 ft) long. There is an

CHILD-FRIENDLY ACCOMMODATION

Jamaica has several all-inclusive hotel chains specifically designed for families – Beaches (Ⓦ www.beaches.com), Franklyn D Resorts (Ⓦ www.fdrholidays.com) and Starfish (Ⓦ www.starfishresorts.com).

⬢ *The smart set: Jamaican schoolchildren*

activity centre with children's games and food stalls. ⓐ Situated near Sandals on Norman Manley Blvd, Negril ① 957 5400
ⓦ www.koolrunnings.com ① 11.00–19.00 Tues–Sun, closed Mon
① Admission charge

Sugar Mill Falls Water park with 'lazy river' for tubing and rafting, several pools, waterfalls, rapids and thrilling slides. ⓐ Rose Hall Resort, A1 coast road east of Montego Bay ① 953 2560
ⓦ www.rosehallresort.com ① 10.00–17.00 daily
① Non-guests can purchase day passes that include all food and drink

White River Valley A leisure park set in hundreds of hectares of lush river valley with adrenalin-fuelled activities such as river-tubing, kayaking and horse riding. ⓐ St Mary's interior, signposted from the A3 coastal highway near Ocho Rios ① 917 3373 ⓦ www.wrvja.com ① 09.00–17.00 daily ① Admission charge

ANIMAL ATTRACTIONS
Alligator Hole The river here is home to a small group of manatees or sea cows. There's a modest display in the visitor centre, and on request (and receipt of a tip) guides will take people out in small boats to try to spot the large, graceful mammals. ⓐ Alligator Hole, South Coast
① No set hours

SEASIDE DANGERS
Although the Caribbean Sea is usually very calm, there are no lifeguards on public beaches and sometimes the water is plagued by shoals of stinging jellyfish (known as stingers in Jamaica). The stings from these can be extremely unpleasant and they should be avoided at all costs. Remember to apply high-factor sun lotion to children's skin – the sun is nearly always very hot. Sun hats and t-shirts give added protection in the water.

Animal Farm Eco-friendly smallholding with exotic birds and snakes, a petting zoo and donkey rides for children. ⓐ Copse, near Lethe, B8 road, St James's interior ❶ 899 0044 Ⓦ www.animalfarmjamaica.com ❶ 10.00–17.00 daily ❶ Admission charge

Black River Safari (see page 47).

Dolphin Cove (see page 24).

🔺 *Dolphin Cove, Ocho Rios, provides great family fun*

Sports & activities

GOLF

Golf is hugely popular in Jamaica and the island boasts half a dozen championship courses. Most of these are concentrated around the Montego Bay suburbs of Ironshore and Rose Hall. There are also courses in Kingston and Negril. Many of the all-inclusive hotels, particularly the Sandals chain (ⓐ www.sandals.com), have their own greens – some of these are very good indeed.

Half Moon Resort ⓐ Ironshore, Montego Bay ❶ 953 3105
ⓦ www.halfmoongolf.com
Ritz-Carlton ⓐ Ironshore, Montego Bay ❶ 518 0174 ⓦ www.ritzcarlton.com
Rose Hall Resort ⓐ Rose Hall, Montego Bay ❶ 953 2650
ⓦ www.rosehallresort.com
Tryall Club ⓐ Tryall, west of Montego Bay ❶ 956 5660
ⓦ www.tryallclub.com

HORSE RIDING

Horse riding is a popular tourist attraction with older children and adults. People especially love the half-day tours, which end up with horse and rider splashing about in the sea. Reputable operators who include this in their itineraries are:
Chukka Caribbean Once the island's best polo field and farm, it is now the HQ for Jamaica's most professional activities tour operator. Horse riding is still offered. ⓐ Chukka Cove Farm, St Ann's Bay ❶ 972 2506
ⓦ www.chukkacaribbean.com
Half Moon Equestrian Centre The island's best riding school, with thoroughbred horses and lessons in polo, dressage and showjumping.
ⓐ Half Moon Resort, Ironshore, Montego Bay ❶ 953 2286
ⓦ www.horsebackridingjamaica.com
Hooves Horseback tours round the Seville Great House and Heritage Park. ⓐ St Ann's Bay, Ocho Rios ❶ 972 0905 ⓦ www.hoovesjamaica.com

COUPLES SWEPT AWAY

The best sports facilities on the island are at Couples Swept Away (☎ 957 4061 ⓦ www.couples.com), an all-inclusive resort in Negril that has a state-of-the-art gym, tennis courts and an Olympic-sized lap pool. Non-guests can purchase day passes to use the resort facilities.

There is a racetrack near Kingston, Caymanas Park (ⓦ www.caymanaspark.com), for those who want to see the professionals at work. Horse racing takes place on Wednesdays and Saturdays.

RAFTING

Taking a rafting tour, reclining on a bamboo raft while your 'captain' poles you slowly down a winding river overhung with trees and tropical

🔺 *Relaxing rafting*

blooms, is one of the most soothing ways to spend a few hours in
Jamaica. Should you feel like a cool drink or a snack, the river banks are
invariably lined with vendors selling provisions as well as souvenirs.

The best of these trips is on the beautiful Rio Grande in Portland,
where Errol Flynn watched banana farmers punting their produce
downriver to the sea and came up with the idea of turning the ride into
a tourist attraction. It's also possible to do shorter tours on the Martha
Brae River at Falmouth, and on the White River just outside Ocho Rios.

Martha Brae – River Raft Ltd ⓐ Rafter's Village – signposted from Water
Square in Falmouth ① 940 6398 ⓦ www.jamaicarafting.com
Rio Grande – Rio Grande Rafting ⓐ Berridale, near Port Antonio
① 913 5434
White River – Calypso Rafting ⓐ Just east of Ocho Rios ① 940 7394
ⓦ www.calypsorafting.com

SPAS

Spas are big business in Jamaica. The best luxury spas are at the Half
Moon (ⓦ www.halfmoon.com), Jamaica Inn (ⓦ www.jamaicainn.com)
and Round Hill (ⓦ www.roundhill.com) hotels. Most offer a range of
treatments using locally sourced products such as pineapple, coffee and
aloe vera. The Rockhouse Hotel in Negril (ⓦ www.rockhouse.com) also
has an attractive spa on its cliff-side property. Traditionalists might want
to visit Bath Fountain Spa (① 703 4345) in Portland or Milk River Spa
(① 902 4657) on the South Coast, both of which claim to have water
with healing qualities and are much patronised by locals.

WATERFALL CLIMBING

Climbing waterfalls is an institution in Jamaica, and though the falls at
Dunn's River (see page 25) are the most obviously impressive, there are a
number of other waterfalls on the island that are far less touristy, with
their own charm. Perhaps the most exhilarating of these is at Mayfield in
the centre-west of the island, which (like Dunn's River) involves climbing
upstream. The more serene pools at Somerset and Reach Falls in Portland
are also great swimming spots, as are those at YS Falls near the South

🔺 *Waterfall climbing is challenging and fun*

Coast. Apart from Reach Falls, these places are managed sites with facilities. Don't forget to take or wear your swimming gear – you're bound to get wet.

Mayfield Falls Entrance to the site is controlled by two separate companies. It's a very isolated spot and the best way to get there is to take a tour with one of several operators who run trips from Negril or Montego Bay. ⓐ Dolphin Head Mountains, Westmoreland
🕐 09.00–18.00 daily ❶ Admission charge
Mayfield Falls ❶ 957 4864 Ⓦ www.mayfieldfalls.com
Riverwalk at Mayfield Falls ❶ 957 3444 Ⓦ www.riverwalkatmayfield.com

Reach Falls Long abandoned to the elements, Reach Falls is now run by the Jamaican government, which has implemented new safety restrictions. The waterfall pools still offer refreshing and calm waters for a swim or splash around. ❶ 993 8863 Ⓦ www.reachfalls.com
🕐 08.30–16.30 Wed–Sun, closed Mon & Tues ❶ Admission charge

Somerset Falls ⓐ St Margaret's Bay, Portland ❶ 913 0046
Ⓦ www.somersetfallsjamaica.com 🕐 09.00–17.00 daily
❶ Admission charge

YS Falls ⓐ Off the A2, inland St Elizabeth Ⓦ www.ysfalls.com
🕐 09.30–15.30 Tues–Sun, closed Mon ❶ Admission charge

WATERSPORTS

With calm sea, excellent visibility and year-round warmth, Jamaica is a great place for watersports. All the big resorts have watersports operators, and activities include waterskiing, parasailing, sailing, snorkelling and scuba diving. Negril has most options (see page 55) and, with its long barrier reef, is the best place in Jamaica to view the tropical underwater world. There is also good scuba diving at Runaway Bay on the north coast. Boston Bay in Portland and Bull Bay near Kingston both have home-grown surf scenes.

Festivals & events

The Jamaica Tourist Board has a comprehensive list of events on its website Ⓦ www.visitjamaica.com

JANUARY
Accompong Maroon Festival Annual celebration of Maroon culture (they were runaway slaves who successfully fought the British in the 18th century and were granted semi-autonomy), with singing, dancing, feasting and traditional ceremonies. ⓐ Accompong, St Elizabeth ⓘ 952 4425 Ⓦ www.visitjamaica.com

FEBRUARY
Bob Marley Birthday Bash, 6 February. Annual celebration, island-wide, of Marley's birthday, with big-name concerts and sound-system jams. ⓐ Bob Marley Museum, Kingston; Nine Mile, St Ann; James Bond Beach, Oracabessa, St Mary; and other locations ⓘ 927 9152 Ⓦ www.bobmarley-foundation.com

APRIL
Carnival A month-long party with steel bands, reggae bands and soca jump-up, which finally ends with a parade through Kingston and the crowning of the Carnival King and Queen. ⓐ Kingston and island-wide ⓘ 969 5520 Ⓦ www.jamaicacarnival.com

Trelawny Yam Festival Four days of yam-filled fun with cook-offs, yam farmer races, yam digging competitions. ⓐ Hague Show Grounds, Trelawny ⓘ 610 0818 Ⓦ www.stea.net

MAY
Calabash Literary Festival A multi-day festival celebrating some of the best Caribbean literature around, complete with guest speakers and participants. ⓐ Treasure Beach, South Coast ⓘ 965 3000 Ⓦ www.calabashfestival.org

JULY

Denbigh Agricultural Show, 1–31 July. Best of island produce and livestock on display. Prizes for Farmer of the Year. ⓐ Denbigh Showground, May Pen, Manchester ⓣ 922 0610

Portland Jerk Festival Annual three-week-long celebration of one of Jamaica's finest foodstuffs, jerk pork. ⓐ Boston Bay, Portland ⓣ 960 7719 ⓦ www.visitjamaica.com

Reggae Sumfest, mid-July. Reggae's biggest celebration, featuring world-class stars. ⓐ Catherine Hall, Montego Bay ⓣ 953 2933 ⓦ www.reggaesumfest.com

🔻 *Carnival in Kingston is an annual highlight*

AUGUST

Independence Day Celebrations, 6 August. Traditional Jonkanoo and modern dancers showcase a cross-section of Jamaican culture. Island-wide events, including a gala street parade in Kingston. ⓐ Island-wide ☎ 926 5726 ⓦ www.jcdc.org.jm

OCTOBER

Best of Jamaica Festival Annual event celebrating all that's good about the island, from food to music. ⓐ Grand Lido Braco Resort & Spa ☎ 954 0019

Old Harbour Fish and Bammy Festival Annual culinary festival and family day out with fish recipes, tasting and storytelling for children. ⓐ Old Harbour, Kingston ☎ 926 3740

Port Antonio International Marlin Competition One of the oldest and most prestigious game-fishing tournaments in the Caribbean. ⓐ Errol Flynn Marina ☎ 715 6044 ⓦ www.errolflynnmarina.com

NOVEMBER

Kingston Restaurant Week Annual event that gives diners the opportunity to taste gourmet food at some of Kingston's finest restaurants for a fraction of the regular cost. ⓐ Kingston ☎ 978 6245 ⓦ www.visitjamaica.com

DECEMBER

Reggae Marathon Coastal run accompanied by pounding reggae music. ⓐ Negril ☎ 922 8677 ⓦ www.reggaemarathon.com

▶ *Keep up to date with what's happening*

Accommodation

Price ratings are based on a double room for one night.
£ = under US$100 **££** = US$100–US$200 **£££** = over US$200

BLUE MOUNTAINS

Mount Edge Guesthouse £ Perched high on a hill in the heart of the Blue
Mountains, this simple, unpretentious guesthouse is the perfect
antidote to Kingston's bustle. ⓐ St Andrew's Parish ⓣ 944 8151
ⓦ www.mountedge.com

KINGSTON

Altamont Court Hotel £–££ All amenities are provided at this spacious,
centrally located hotel. ⓐ 1–5 Altamont Terrace, New Kingston
ⓣ 929 5931 ⓦ www.altamontcourt.com

Strawberry Hill £££ This beautifully designed and classy hotel in the Blue
Mountains overlooks Kingston. ⓐ Irish Town, Blue Mountains
ⓣ 944 8400 ⓦ www.strawberryhillresort.com

MONTEGO BAY

Casa Blanca Beach Hotel ££ Fantastically sited hotel with spacious,
breezy rooms and a lovely beach. Air conditioning, TV and all mod cons.
ⓐ Gloucester Ave ⓣ 952 0720 ⓦ www.casablancajamaica.com

Doctor's Cave Beach Hotel ££ Comfortable family-run hotel with pool
terrace, bar and live music nights. ⓐ Gloucester Ave ⓣ 952 4355
ⓦ www.doctorscave.com

NEGRIL

Chippewa Village £–££ Friendly resort with eclectic décor and
wide range of accommodation. ⓐ Norman Manley Blvd ⓣ 957 4676
ⓦ www.chippewavillageresort.com

Rockhouse ££ This gorgeous cliff-side hotel has an excellent restaurant and spa on-site. ⓐ West End Rd ⓣ 957 4373 ⓦ www.rockhousehotel.com

Idle Awhile £££ Luxurious and attractive rooms right on the beach. ⓐ Norman Manley Blvd ⓣ 957 3303 ⓦ www.idleawhile.com

OCHO RIOS
Little Shaw Park Guest House £ Simple, clean and friendly guesthouse. ⓐ 21 Shaw Park Rd ⓣ 974 2177 ⓦ www.littleshawparkguesthouse.com

Rooms £ Centrally located, clean and comfortable, this hotel is run by the SuperClubs chain. ⓐ Main St ⓣ 925 0925 ⓦ www.superclubs.com

Jamaica Inn £££ Classy, old-fashioned hotel with elegant rooms, lovely gardens and private beach. ⓐ Main St ⓣ 974 2514 ⓦ www.jamaicainn.com

PORT ANTONIO
Ivanhoe's Guest House £ Excellent, spotlessly clean guesthouse in heart of old Port Antonio. ⓐ 9 Queen St, Titchfield Peninsula ⓣ 993 3043

Great Huts £–££ This eco resort with painted tents, tree houses and wooden cabins is right next to Boston Bay. ⓐ Boston Bay ⓣ 993 8888 ⓦ www.greathuts.com

SOUTH COAST
Villa Bella £ Quaint hotel with antique furnishings and old-style hospitality. ⓐ Christiana, Manchester ⓣ 964 2243 ⓦ www.hotelvillabella.com

Jake's ££–£££ Lively and bohemian seaside hideaway at the heart of Treasure Beach. ⓐ Calabash Bay, Treasure Beach ⓣ 965 3000 ⓦ www.jakeshotel.com

Preparing to go

GETTING THERE
By air

The best way to get to Jamaica is either with a scheduled flight or on a package holiday. Air Jamaica no longer flies between the island and the UK. Instead British Airways flies to Kingston from Gatwick and Virgin flies to Montego Bay from Gatwick. Flight times are nine hours. Air Jamaica has frequent hopper flights between the two international airports – the flight takes 30 minutes. The site 🌐 www.cheapflights.co.uk highlights last-minute offers.

Many people are aware that air travel emits CO_2, which contributes to climate change. You may be interested in the possibility of lessening the environmental impact of your flight through the charity Climate Care, which offsets your CO_2 by funding environmental projects around the world. Visit 🌐 www.jpmorganclimatecare.com

Air Jamaica ☎ 020 7590 3600 🌐 www.airjamaica.com
British Airways ☎ 0870 850 9850 🌐 www.ba.com
Virgin Atlantic ☎ 0870 380 2007 🌐 www.virgin-atlantic.com

Package holidays

Dozens of package tour operators offer holidays in Jamaica and often have great deals with flights, accommodation and board included. In low season it's sometimes cheaper to buy a package holiday than to buy the flight on its own. Try Googling 'Jamaica tour operators' for a comprehensive list.

Caribtours ☎ 020 7751 0660 🌐 www.caribtours.co.uk
Complete Caribbean ☎ 01423 531031 🌐 www.completecaribbean.co.uk
Expressions Holidays 🌐 www.expressionsholidays.co.uk
Thomas Cook ☎ 0870 895 0055 🌐 www.thomascook.com

High season in the Caribbean is from December to April. May to June and September to November are low season; the months of September

TRAVEL INSURANCE

Travel insurance is essential. Holiday cover should include theft, loss and illness or injury. Make sure that your insurer will repatriate you if necessary and that the single-item limit on goods is high enough for you to be able to afford a replacement. Extra premiums might be needed for 'dangerous sports' – in Jamaica these might be scuba diving or white-water rafting.

and October are usually very rainy but this is the time to bag a bargain by tracking down cheap flights and accommodation. The months of July and August are when Europeans tend to head to Jamaica, and so they are fairly busy.

TOURISM AUTHORITY

The Jamaica Tourist Board has an office in London and has a useful website. ⓐ 1–2 Prince Consort Rd, London SW7 2BZ ⓣ 020 7225 9090 ⓦ www.visitjamaica.com

BEFORE YOU LEAVE

There are several things to be aware of as you start to plan your holiday. No vaccinations are required to enter Jamaica, though you might want to consider hepatitis A, tetanus and typhoid if you're going to hike or swim in Jamaica's rivers. A simple first-aid kit is handy, containing plasters, antiseptic cream, insect repellent, bite-relief cream, painkillers, upset stomach remedies and rehydration powder. If you're taking prescription medicines, make sure you'll have enough to last the holiday, since they may not be available on the island. Those thinking about engaging in sexual activity should take condoms – the local brands are not reliable. It is also worth having a dental check-up before you leave the UK.

In the popular winter months it can be cool in the evenings and cold in the high Blue Mountains. Take a jacket or cardigan for nights out.

Jamaica is tropical, which means it rains a lot – take a raincoat and/or umbrella for sudden showers.

ENTRY FORMALITIES

All foreign citizens require a passport and a return or onward ticket. Make sure that your passport has at least six months left to run on it. Citizens of the US, Canada, the UK, Australia and New Zealand are allowed to stay for six months and no visa is required (residents of other countries are allowed to remain for 30 or 90 days; stays longer than this will require a visa). Visitors are asked to fill out an entry form on the plane. It is essential that you fill in the name and address of your hotel – if you don't, you may have a long delay at immigration. Officials often also ask for proof of funds.

Foreign visitors are allowed to bring in 200 cigarettes, 25 cigars, 1 litre of spirits and 2 bottles of wine.

MONEY

The unit of currency is the Jamaican dollar (J$), called the 'jay' by locals. Banknotes are in denominations of J$1,000, J$500, J$100 and J$50. Note that the J$1,000 and J$100 bills look very similar and it's easy to mix them up if you're not careful. Coins, called cents, are in denominations of J$20, J$10, J$5 and J$1.

The US dollar has long served as an unofficial parallel currency and all hotels, restaurants and attractions geared for tourists accept them. Smaller places – bars, markets and cafés – often do not take them, so you should always carry a small supply of Jamaican currency.

Cashpoints or ATMs are widely available in most resorts and at petrol stations. ATMs in the larger resorts dispense US dollars as well as Jamaican currency – look out for Cool Cash outlets. Traveller's cheques can be changed in banks, and those in US dollar denominations can also be used for some purchases. Major credit cards are accepted in hotels and many restaurants and shops in major towns.

CLIMATE

Jamaica has a tropical climate with an average year-round air (and sea) temperature of 27°C (80°F). Winters are mostly dry and slightly cooler than summers and there is a welcome breeze to alleviate the heat. September and October are the most humid months, with much more rainfall – in October this reaches 178 mm (7 in), which is seven times greater than the rainfall in January. October is also the month most prone to hurricanes.

BAGGAGE ALLOWANCE

Standard baggage allowance is 23 kg (51 lb) per person for checked-in baggage, and airlines now enforce this rigidly. If you have more, you will have to pay a hefty excess baggage charge. British Airways only allows one piece of checked-in luggage per person. Travellers are also only allowed one piece of carry-on luggage (this includes laptops), which must measure no more than 50 cm by 40 cm by 20 cm (20 in by 15¼ in by 7¾ in) and again, bags are expected to meet regulations. Increased security regulations mean that all liquid items including water and make-up as well as sharp objects (penknives, scissors) cannot be carried on board and should be packed in check-in baggage.

During your stay

AIRPORTS

There are two international airports in Jamaica, both named after former Prime Ministers.

Sangster International Airport in Montego Bay (☎ 952 3124
🌐 www.mbjairport.com) is the gateway to the north coast and to the west side of the island. There is no public transport from the airport into the city. Most hotels offer a free pick-up if you've booked in advance. Otherwise there are numerous taxis outside (you can pay in US dollars – make sure you agree the price first). There are plenty of car rental agencies at the airport, an ATM and currency-exchange counter, and a tourist information booth.

Norman Manley International Airport in Kingston (☎ 924 8452
🌐 www.nmia.aero) is useful if you're travelling to the Blue Mountains, Portland or the South Coast. City bus number 98 passes the airport, though you'll need to know the city if you take it. There are taxis, car rental agencies and a currency-exchange booth.

COMMUNICATIONS

Jamaica has been revolutionised by the arrival of mobile phones. Payphones, scarcely used these days by Jamaicans, do still exist and you'll have to buy a phonecard from a supermarket or petrol station.

If you have a tri-band phone, the easiest – and cheapest – way to make phone calls is to buy a Digicel (☎ 960 2696
🌐 www.digiceljamaica.com) prepaid SIM card from any one of numerous outlets island-wide. This is then topped up by buying Flex cards or credit from supermarkets, service stations and many other locations.

Big resorts and hotels in Jamaica rent phones to guests for a small fee, as do both Cable & Wireless and Digicel. Some visitors use international calling cards – as good as any is the local prepaid World Talk, widely available all over Jamaica.

There are internet cafés in most Jamaican towns, though hourly rates are high. A number of hotels now offer free internet facilities to guests; the growing trend is to establish wireless zones in the larger resort hotels.

POSTAL SERVICES

There are post offices in most towns in Jamaica, open 09.00–17.00 Monday to Friday, but leave at least ten days for mail to reach Europe or North America. Stamps, sold at post offices and in hotels, cost J$50 for a postcard to anywhere in the world. Rates for international letters and parcels are available online at ⓦ www.jamaicapost.gov.jm

CUSTOMS

Jamaica is typically Caribbean in that it has few formal customs. Time is extremely elastic and the much used expression 'soon come' means that things will happen eventually. Visitors should get used to long waits in local restaurants and appointments rarely being kept on the dot.

However, Jamaica is also a very religious and traditional place and good manners are hugely appreciated. Jamaicans usually refer to strangers by their titles and surnames (first names are for close friends and family) and old ladies are called 'Miss'. Be careful about discussing religion if you're an atheist – even the coolest of youths will be shocked

INTERNATIONAL TELEPHONE CODES

There are no regional codes in Jamaica. The country code is 876. If you're calling Jamaica from abroad dial 001 876 followed by the phone number.

When dialling abroad from Jamaica, the following codes are required:
Australia 00 + 61 + city code (minus the first zero)
Ireland 00 + 353 + city code (minus the first zero)
New Zealand 00 + 64 + city code (minus the first zero)
South Africa 00 + 27 + city code
UK 00 + 44 + city code (minus the first zero)
US & Canada 00 + 1 + area code

To speak to an operator in Jamaica dial 113.

at your lack of belief in God. Homosexuality is illegal and highly disapproved of – homosexuals should not display affection in public.

Jamaicans are incredibly direct people. Tourists are often shocked by being called 'fatty' (not an insult in Jamaica, where the more flesh the better) or 'whitey'. This is not intended to offend. A sense of humour goes a long way in these circumstances – and in general on the island.

DRESS CODES

In the beach resorts, Jamaicans are used to tourists in few clothes and won't comment, though they might stare at scantily dressed women, in spite of the fact that Jamaican women often wear little more than batty riders (hot pants) and a bikini top. Female tourists should avoid trying to imitate this look or risk getting into trouble with the local guys.

On the other hand, business wear is still very formal. In the city or large towns try to dress with some decorum. Topless or nude bathing is not customary, though the private beaches of all-inclusive resorts all have nude bathing sections.

Jamaicans take dressing to impress very seriously. A night out means slinky dresses, sharp suits and lots of 'bling'. If you turn up for an occasion in jeans and a t-shirt you may displease your hosts.

ELECTRICITY

The island runs on 110 volts with flat two-pin sockets.

EMERGENCIES

EMERGENCY NUMBERS
Ambulance 110
Police 119

Hospitals

If you have a medical emergency it's best to get your hotel reception to help you out – most hotels have a list of local doctors, though they're not

free. Generally, public hospitals in Jamaica are not good.
There are two decent public hospitals in Kingston:

Kingston Public Hospital @ North St ☎ 922 0210

University Hospital @ Mona ☎ 927 1620

Recommended private hospitals:

Medical Associates @ 18 Tangerine Place, New Kingston ☎ 926 1400

Nuttall Memorial @ 6 Caledonia Ave, New Kingston ☎ 926 7401

There is also a decent public hospital in Montego Bay:

Cornwall Regional Hospital @ Mount Salem ☎ 952 5100

Montego Bay also has a state-of-the-art private hospital that can deal
with dental emergencies as well and has its own ambulance:

MoBay Hope Medical Clinic @ Half Moon Shopping Village, Rose Hall
☎ 953 3649

Embassies

British High Commission @ 28 Trafalgar Rd, Kingston ☎ 510 0700
🌐 www.ukinjamaica.fco.gov.uk

Canadian High Commission @ 3 West Kings House Rd, Kingston
☎ 926 1500 🌐 www.canadainternational.gc.ca/jamaica-jamaique

US Embassy @ 142 Old Hope Rd, Kingston 6 ☎ 1-800 572 7780
🌐 http://kingston.usembassy.gov

GETTING AROUND

Car hire

Major international car rental companies have offices at both airports –
Montego Bay has the most choice – but rates are high. Drivers must be
over 21 and have a current driving licence.

Driving is on the left. Speed limits are set at 50 km/h (30 mph) in
towns and on minor roads and 80 km/h (50 mph) on major roads. The
new highways are excellent, but in other parts of the island the roads are
abysmal (for instance in the Blue Mountains and the Rio Grande valley).
Jamaicans are reckless drivers, often overtaking on blind corners. Watch for
people, as well as goats and chickens, wandering on the roads, particularly
at night. Additionally Jamaicans rarely dip their headlights. Tooting horns

are a constant background noise on the roads – they mean anything from 'hello' to warning of police checks or accidents ahead.

Internal flights

The domestic airline Air Jamaica (📞 922 3460 🌐 www.airjamaica.com) runs a frequent shuttle service between Montego Bay and Kingston. Charter service International Airlink (📞 1-888-airlink 🌐 www.intlairlink.com) operates regular flights to Negril and Ocho Rios and can also be chartered to Port Antonio.

Public transport

Jamaican buses, which take the form of small white minibuses, are crowded, hot and noisy. There are no real timetables (they leave when full) and drivers are reckless. One exception is the Knutsford Express (📞 971 1822 🌐 www.knutsfordexpress.com), which runs an air-conditioned coach between the Montego Bay bus park and New Kingston twice daily. Fares are less than US$25 one way and include newspapers and bottled water. For short distances, locals take route taxis, cars that drive set routes and stop when they're flagged down. There are no trains.

Taxis

Taxis are ubiquitous – look out for red licence plates. They're not a cheap option, but you can usually negotiate the price before you set off. Try to use JUTA (Jamaican Union of Travellers Association) taxis: they are more expensive but are properly regulated and very reliable.

JUTA:
Kingston 📞 927 4534   Negril 📞 957 9197
Montego Bay 📞 952 0813   Ocho Rios 📞 974 2292

HEALTH, SAFETY & CRIME

Healthwise, Jamaica has few hazards. Tap water is safe to drink and food is generally properly prepared. Mosquitoes and sand flies are prevalent in the humid summer.

AIDS is rife, and visitors should *never* have unprotected sex. Private healthcare is widely available (if you need a doctor, ask at your hotel) and good. Costs are similar to those at home. The island's best private health centre is the MoBay Hope Medical Clinic (953 3649) in Montego Bay.

Crime levels are highly exaggerated. Generally Jamaica is safe, though tourists in the big resorts should take the usual precautions when out and about: don't flash wads of money or wear expensive jewellery; don't put your handbag down; don't wander round downtown at night; don't jump into an unmarked taxi. Special tourist police (in maroon berets and navy-blue uniforms) patrol beaches and streets and have the power to fine hustlers who bother tourists.

MEDIA

Leading newspapers include the *Daily Gleaner* (www.jamaica-gleaner.com) and the *Jamaica Observer* (www.jamaicaobserver.com) morning dailies. *Jamaica Tourist* (www.jamaicatourist.net) is a free newspaper with features and listings. The resorts sell a wide range of international newspapers.

The BBC World Service is broadcast in Jamaica, as is BBC Caribbean (www.bbc.co.uk/caribbean), which is a good source of local and international news. Of the home-grown radio stations, the most popular is music station Irie FM (www.iriefm.net). Power 106 (www.go-jamaica.com/power) broadcasts a range of excellent talk shows.

Most hotels offer a range of cable TV channels.

OPENING HOURS

Banks open on Monday to Thursday between 09.00 and 14.00 and on Friday from 09.00 until 15.00 or 16.00. Shops open on Monday to Saturday from 08.30 to 17.00 or 18.00 and often close for lunch. Offices are open for business during the week from 09.00 to 16.00 or 17.00.

RELIGION

Most Jamaicans are Anglican Christians. A small minority are Roman Catholics, Rastafarians, Jewish, Muslim or Hindu.

TIME DIFFERENCES

Jamaica is on Eastern Standard Time and does not adjust for Daylight Saving Time. It is five hours behind the UK (six from spring to autumn) and six behind most of Europe (seven from spring to autumn). It's on the same time as New York in the US (one hour behind from spring to autumn) and Toronto in Canada. It's 15 hours behind Sydney in Australia and 17 hours behind Auckland, New Zealand.

TIPPING

Waiters and staff in the large resorts are used to tips of 10 to 15 per cent. The all-inclusive hotels forbid tipping. In local eating joints, tipping is not expected, and nor do taxi drivers expect tips.

TOILETS

Public toilets are non-existent in Jamaica. If you get caught short, you'll have to beg café owners or barmen to let you use their facilities.

TRAVELLERS WITH DISABILITIES

Large and medium-sized hotels have ramps for wheelchair access, as do most of the all-inclusive resorts. The JTB (Jamaica Tourist Board) has a list of hotels with wheelchair ramps. Otherwise Jamaica is not especially well set up for travellers with disabilities, though locals are usually very good at helping those with little mobility.

For further information contact:

Disabled Peoples International North America and the Caribbean
ⓐ Potters Main Rd, St John's, Antigua ⓣ +1 (268) 461 7260
ⓦ http://caribbean.dpi.org
Jamaica Council for the Handicapped ⓐ 92 Hanover St, Kingston ⓣ 922 6304
The United Kingdom's Disabled People's Council ⓐ Litchurch Plaza,
Litchurch Lane, Derby DE24 8AA ⓣ 01332 295551 ⓦ www.bcodp.org.uk

Useful websites:
In the UK ⓦ www.accessibletravel.co.uk
In the US ⓦ www.access-able.com

ACKNOWLEDGEMENTS

The publishers would like to thank the following individuals and organisations for providing copyright photographs for this book:
Polly Rodger Brown pages 13, 85;
Pictures Colour Library pages 5, 26, 111;
World Pictures/Photoshot pages 8, 61, 106;
all the rest, Mark Bassett

Project editor: Tom Willsher
Proofreader: Ian Faulkner
Layout: Donna Pedley

Send your thoughts to
books@thomascook.com

- **Found a beach bar, peaceful stretch of sand or must-see sight that we don't feature?**

- **Like to tip us off about any information that needs a little updating?**

- **Want to tell us what you love about this handy little guidebook and more importantly how we can make it even handier?**

Then here's your chance to tell all! Send us ideas, discoveries and recommendations today and then look out for your valuable input in the next edition of this title.

Send an email to the above address or write to:
HotSpots Series Editor, Thomas Cook Publishing,
Thomas Cook Business Park, PO Box 227, Coningsby Road,
Peterborough PE3 8SB, UK